Charles A. Row

The Principles of Modern Pantheistic and Atheistic Philosophy

as exemplified in the last works of Strauss and others - being a paper read

before the Victoria Institute, or Philosophical Society of Great Britain, 13th

April, 1874

Charles A. Row

The Principles of Modern Pantheistic and Atheistic Philosophy
as exemplified in the last works of Strauss and others - being a paper read before
the Victoria Institute, or Philosophical Society of Great Britain, 13th April, 1874

ISBN/EAN: 9783337235642

Printed in Europe, USA, Canada, Australia, Japan

Cover: Foto ©Thomas Meinert / pixelio.de

More available books at **www.hansebooks.com**

THE PRINCIPLES OF MODERN

PANTHEISTIC AND ATHEISTIC

PHILOSOPHY:

AS EXEMPLIFIED IN THE LAST WORKS OF STRAUSS AND OTHERS.

BY

REV. C. A. ROW, M.A.

PREBENDARY OF ST. PAUL'S.

WITH SOME REMARKS ON THE SUBJECT

BY THE REV. PROFESSOR CHALLIS, M.A. F.R.S. F.R.A.S.

REPRINTED FROM THE JOURNAL OF THE TRANSACTIONS OF THE VICTORIA INSTITUTE, OR PHILOSOPHICAL SOCIETY OF GREAT BRITAIN.

LONDON:
(Published for the Institute)
ROBERT HARDWICKE, 192, PICCADILLY.
1874.

PANTHEISTIC AND ATHEISTIC PHILOSOPHY.

THE following passage from the *Autobiography of the late Mr. J. S. Mill* demands the earnest attention of all those who believe that there is a personal God, who is the moral governor of the universe:—"The world would be astonished if it knew how great a proportion of its brightest ornaments—of those most distinguished even in popular estimation for wisdom and virtue—are complete sceptics on religion, many of them refraining from avowal, less from personal considerations, than from a conscientious, though now in my opinion most mistaken apprehension, lest by speaking out what may tend to weaken existing beliefs, and by consequence, as they suppose, existing restraints, they should do harm rather than good."

2. The first question which strikes the mind on reading this passage is, is the assertion true, "that a large proportion of the 'world's brightest ornaments' are complete sceptics on religion"? If so, it is of the most serious import. Mr. Mill has probably exerted a greater influence in the higher regions of thought than any writer of the existing generation. No holder of his philosophy can any longer entertain a doubt that certain portions of it are the philosophy of scepticism. The peculiar idiosyncrasies of mind which the Autobiography discloses, may have led Mr. Mill somewhat to over-estimate the sceptical tendencies of others. Yet the large number of writings, which have been recently published, of a similar tendency, is a sufficiently clear evidence that the principles of a pantheistic or atheistic philosophy are widely diffused among cultivated minds. Strauss, in his recent work, distinctly affirms that he is only acting as the spokesman of a wide range of pantheistic thought.

3. I quite concur with Mr. Mill in opinion, that the time is come for speaking out plainly. In fact, unless morality is nothing better than expediency, there never has been a time when it has been right to profess adhesion to a system of thought, which in secret we utterly despise. I fully concede that theologians no less than philosophers would do well to act

on this opinion, and not to have an exoteric doctrine for the vulgar, and an esoteric one for themselves. But it is with the latter that I am now dealing. A sound philosophy requires, that the too frequent example of the ancient philosopher, who acted the part of the high priest of the god whose moral character he despised, and whose existence he disbelieved, should be utterly repudiated. What can be more degrading than the spectacle of an atheist Cæsar, dressed in the pontifical robes, uttering solemn vows to Jupiter in the Capitol? Persons capable of acting such a part must have a supreme contempt for the vulgar herd of humanity; and are at one in principle with the priests whose conduct they denounce. It is satisfactory to be informed that in the opinion of Mr. J. S. Mill, his father's prudential principle of not avowing his opinions to the world "was attended with *some* moral disadvantages." The italics are ours; in place of "some" we would read "great."

4. Before entering on the consideration of some of the principles of pantheistic and atheistic philosophy, to which I propose drawing attention in the present paper, it will be necessary to state what Atheism, as held by men of culture, really means. The son's account of the character of his father's atheism will clearly define its nature. "Finding," says Mr. J. S. Mill, "no halting-place in Theism, he yielded to the conviction, that concerning the origin of things nothing whatever can be known. This is the only correct statement of his opinion, for dogmatic Atheism he looked on as absurd, as most of those whom the world have considered atheists have always done." Atheism, therefore, as a philosophic theory, does not consist in the denial of the being of a God, but in the affirmation that there is no evidence that there is one. The moral value of the distinction between these two positions is *nil*, but the intellectual one is great, for it frees him who entertains it from the necessity of proving a negative.

5. The following is worthy of quotation, as an illustration of the nature of the elder Mill's atheistic reasonings. "He impressed upon me from the first that the manner in which the world came into existence was a subject about which nothing was known; that the question, 'Who made me?' cannot be answered, because we have no experience or authentic information from which to answer it; and that the answer only throws the difficulty a step further back, since the question immediately presents itself, 'Who made God?'" It is almost incredible that such reasoning could have commended itself as valid to a man of the mental acuteness of the elder Mill; and it is

quite a relief to be informed by the son that his father's atheism was rather moral than intellectual.

6. I now proceed to examine some of the philosophic principles on which modern Pantheism and Atheism are based; and, first, their principle of causation. It is an accepted dogma of the Positive philosophy that a cause is nothing but an invariable sequence between an antecedent and a consequent, and that the notion of any efficiency in the cause to produce its effect is a fancy which has been exploded by the discoveries of physical science. This opinion is the natural outcome of a philosophy which teaches that the whole of objective nature, and even the fundamental principles of the mind, are nothing else but a bare succession of phenomena; and that a knowledge of any truth objectively valid for all time and space is unattainable by man.

7. It strikes one at first sight as a strong objection against such a system of philosophy that language has been formed on the assumption that it is not true. Its forms embody the universal experience of mankind, and have grown out of that experience. Now, nothing is more certain than that whenever we use words denoting causation we mean by them something very different from the mere invariable following of a consequent on an antecedent. If this is the true idea of a cause, nothing is more misleading than human language; for it is impossible to express the conceptions of this philosophy in it except by using it in a non-natural sense. One of the first duties which it owes to truth is to revolutionize human language, for, in its present forms, it is incapable of being the vehicle of accurate thought. If, therefore, this philosophy is a true representation of ultimate realities, one of its first duties is to attempt to construct a language capable of expressing them. At present it is a strong argument against the truth of this system of philosophy, that a few philosophers are committed to a particular theory on the one side; and, on the contrary, is the universal experience of mankind, as testified by the fundamental structure and the forms of language.

8. This philosophy also carries out to its utmost limits the doctrine of the relativity of human knowledge. Of this Mr. Mill is one of the strongest advocates; he even considers it possible that in some distant region of the universe, two and two may make five. Beyond this, it seems impossible to push the doctrine in question. Such an affirmation is a strange one to be made by a philosophy, which professes to ground all human knowledge on experience, for it certainly transcends all experience. Next, it is directly contradictory to the principles of at least one science. Astronomy has penetrated into regions of the universe immeasurably

remote. Its calculations are based on the assumption that in the remotest regions two and two make four; and if any region existed in which they did not make four but five, the whole of its apparatus of calculation would be subverted. Next, the assertion that two and two make four and not five, is a truth self-evident to the mind as soon as it is capable of comprehending the terms. It is marvellous that any man should have made such a statement. What is two? $1 + 1$. What is four? $1 + 1 + 1 + 1$. What is five? $1 + 1 + 1 + 1 + 1$. It is therefore evident that the proposition $2 + 2$, i. e. $(1+1) + (1+1)$ must make 4, i.e. $1 + 1 + 1 + 1$, and not five, i.e. $1 + 1 + 1 + 1 + 1$, must be valid for all thought, all space, and all time, and that to affirm the contrary is to assert the possibility of contradictions being true. It follows, therefore, that all our knowledge is not relative.

9. If all our knowledge is only relative and phenomenal, on what does our belief in the existence of an external universe rest? It will be answered, on experience. But what renders such experience valid? How do we know that any sensation or mental conception has anything to correspond to it outside our minds? This cannot be the result of experience alone, for all that we are actually cognizant of are certain mental states. Yet our belief in the reality of an external world is so strong, that it cannot be shaken by any amount of reasoning. Moreover, it is no mere result of a balance of probabilities, but it is a firm and ultimate persuasion, on which it is impossible to avoid acting. If the alternative of idealism or materialism were presented to our minds as a matter of abstract reasoning, the balance of the evidence would turn in favour of idealism. Still we cannot help believing in the reality of an external world, and we shall continue to do so despite of all philosophy.

10. To say that this belief is derived from experience is to beg the question at issue, because there must be something to give validity to the primary experience; and which has enabled us to infer from some primary act of sensation, the externality of the cause producing it. The only possible account of our belief is, that there must be some principle in the mind (be it what it may) independent of sensation, which compels us to believe in the externality of the cause producing it. This power may be called into activity by an act of sensation; but it is impossible that it can be its mere result. Such beliefs the mind pronounces to have a universal validity. Of a similar character are the great truths which lie at the foundations of our reasonings. It is impossible to conceive of them as true in one place and not true in another. It is impossible, therefore,

to view them as the mere result of our experience of phenomena.

11. Of a similar nature must be our idea of causation. Its primary conception is unquestionably derived from our own self-consciousness. Experience may aid in its evolution; but it is impossible that it can have originated it. All that we can have experience of is, a succession of events one following the other in which we observe no variation. We advance one point beyond experience, when we arrive at the conception of an invariable succession. Yet there are innumerable successions which are in no sense causes. It may not be possible fully to develop the idea in the formal intellect. But we know it, we believe in it, we feel it; it lies at the foundation of our reason.

12. But further, it is not strictly true, that whenever there is an invariable antecedent and consequent, the one is the cause of the other: day and night stand to each other in the order of an invariable antecedent and consequent, and they must have done so from their first origin. Yet the absurdity of affirming that the one is the cause of the other is apparent. Many instances of invariable antecedents and consequents exist which it would be absurd to designate causes. It follows, therefore, that a cause must be something more than an antecedent, followed by an invariable consequent.

13. Our primary idea of causation has been unquestionably derived from our own self-consciousness, and has thence been transferred to the forces of external nature. Our conception of ourselves as voluntary originators of actions constitutes our only adequate idea of a cause. The consciousness that we are capable of originating actions forms one of the highest of our certitudes. It is one which is anterior to all reasoning, and forms the groundwork of its possibility. We know that our volition sets an entire chain of antecedents and consequents in action. We are certain that they derived their impulse from a voluntary act of our own, without which they would have had no existence.

14. Let me illustrate this by an example. Let us suppose a city to be blown to pieces by applying a match to a barrel of powder in a large magazine. It is incorrect to say that the match is the cause of the explosion. The true cause was the voluntary act of the agent who applied the match. No other of the agencies adequately satisfies the idea. But are the other unconscious forces which bear their part in the work of destruction nothing else but bare antecedents and consesequents? Does it satisfy our conception of a physical force,

8

when it is in active energy, to describe it as such, and nothing more? I contend that it does not. What follows the ignition of the match, and its application to the barrel? The calling into activity of a number of forces, which are adequate to effect their destructive work. Are they nothing but antecedents? The mind refuses to regard a bare antecedent as fulfilling its conception of a force.

15. What is the real state of the facts? A volition determines on the action; and the understanding suggests the means adequate to accomplish it. The volition sets in action the bodily apparatus of nerves, muscles, &c. These kindle the match by friction. The match ignites the powder in the barrel, and liberates its forces; the barrel, the entire magazine. The explosion calls into activity a terrific force: this occasions a concussion of the atmosphere: the concussion effects the details of the work of destruction.

16. In a popular sense all these things are designated causes. Some of them are evidently more than bare antecedents. They are forces in energy. The conception of such a force implies the presence of a power adequate to effectuate the result. If it be urged that the force and the result are necessarily united together as antecedent and consequent, a true philosophy is bound to account for that necessity. It cannot be given by experience; and is something different from a mere phenomenon. If we affirm that the necessity is the result of a primal law, then we have arrived at the existence of a truth which must have a universal validity independently of phenomena.

17. Now, a necessary law cannot be arrived at as a bare result of experience, or have any place in a phenomenal universe. It is only conceivable as inherent in something underlying phenomena. It follows, therefore, that whenever a pantheistic or atheistic philosophy postulates the existence of necessary law, without which it cannot advance a single step in creating the universe without a God, it is compelled to admit the existence of truths valid for all space and all time; and thus to subvert the foundation on which it rests. How can we affirm that such exist in a universe in which we can know nothing but phenomena? If there be none other, philosophy must be impossible.

18. A system which refuses to take cognizance of the facts of consciousness, and to probe them to the bottom, must be necessarily one-sided. It is true that they cannot be weighed in scales, or measured by the finest instruments; which a certain class of thinkers assert to be the only criterion of truth.

Yet we can have no higher certitudes than these. If they are not certitudes, none other can be; for unless they are such, experimental knowledge is impossible.

19. But further : while this philosophy affirms that all our knowledge is the result of experience, and that we have only experience of phenomena, a modern form of it endeavours to escape from the difficulties in which it is encircled, by allowing that the experience may not be that of the individual, but the inherited experience of the race. Accordingly, it affirms that that portion of our knowledge which appears to transcend experience is really the result of a transmitted experience, derived from a long line of ancestors. How this relieves us from the difficulty it is difficult to see.

20. To deal with such a question adequately would render it necessary to discuss the relation between subject and object. This alone might well occupy an entire volume. Still, without entering into these depths, there are a few obvious facts which will be sufficient to test the truth of the position which this philosophy seeks to establish.

21. First. The assertion that all our knowledge is phenomenal, and that we are incapable of arriving at any knowledge of universal objective validity, is absolutely suicidal. The most sceptical philosophy would be still-born, unless there was some one truth which is not of this description,—viz., that which affirms the universal validity of its own assertions. Unless it was objectively valid, universal scepticism must be the result ; otherwise it might be true in one part of the universe, and not true in another. So, again, the affirmation of our reason that one of two contradictory propositions must be false, must be a knowledge which transcends experience, and be universally valid. To affirm the contrary would destroy the basis on which even the most sceptical philosophy must rest. Again : it is affirmed by a popular form of philosophy, that all propositions which transcend the phenomenal are unknowable ; into which region it banishes the conception of a God. If it be so, it follows that this proposition must possess a universal objective validity independent of the subject which affirms it. Some knowledge, therefore, must be attainable which transcends experience. Even Pyrrhonism is compelled to affirm that one truth exists which is universally valid,—viz., that all truth is impossible.

22. When God is banished by this philosophy into the regions of the unknowable, it confounds under a common name a number of conceptions entirely distinct ; and boldly affirms that they all alike transcend the powers of rational thought.

The only ones which do so are those, the truth of which is positively unthinkable. Others vary greatly in distinctness and adequacy; but the fact that we habitually think and reason on them proves that they lie within the limits of rational inquiry.

23. Again, as far as this question is concerned, to affirm that many of our certitudes are not the result of the experience of the individual, but of his remote ancestors, is to transfer thedifficulty, but not to solve it. I ask, on what did the primary experience of our remote ancestors rest? What gave it validity? However small its results, it must have possessed some principle, which rendered it possible. Let us suppose, for the sake of argument, that the affirmation, that things which are equal to the same thing, are equal to each other, is the result of a gradually accumulated experience, which, after repeated transmissions, now exhibits itself in our minds in the form of an intuition. Does this account of it as the result of a transmitted experience give any account of the primary conception of equality; or of the affirmation, that when two things are equal to the same thing they must be equal to one another? Does it inform us, how the power of comparison between two equal things originated? The being who could thus compare must have been separated from one who could not—not by a small interval, but by a wide and deep gulf. Will the tracing it through myriads of years help us to dispense with a commencement of the conception? The only possible account of the matter is, that there must exist some fundamental principle in the mind, which enables us to see that it must be objectively valid for all time and all space. I do not deny that experience may be the medium through which such a power may be called from a dormant into an active state. Yet this does not affect the proof that some truth must transcend experience. Were it not so, all universal affirmations would be impossible.

24. Further: some principle must exist in the mind, which is the foundation of its conviction that past events, when the conditions are the same, will repeat themselves in the future. Unless this be so, the affirmation of universal law, embracing alike the past, the present and the future, would be invalid. It is impossible that it can be given by experience alone.

25. It is evident that every affirmation respecting the future must transcend experience; for experience can be only of the present and the past. The future has not yet existed, and therefore experience of it is impossible. How, then, have we arrived at the belief that the future will be like the past? To put the question into a concrete form. How are we justified

in inferring, because the sun has risen every day of our past lives, that it will rise again to morrow? It has been urged that our experience of the past, and that of others, justifies us in inferring that the future will be like the past; that the past events of our lives were once future, and that from their having taken place, we are justified in inferring that similar ones will take place hereafter.

26. It is evident that this belief does not in any respect participate in an axiomatic character. The contrary of it is quite conceivable. Thus we are fully able to conceive the possibility that the sun may not rise to-morrow; though we feel perfectly certain that it will. So firm is our conviction that events, under precisely similar circumstances, will reproduce themselves, that it forms the foundation on which all human activity rests.

27. Is it possible, then, that our experience that past events have repeated themselves under similar conditions, can account for our belief that they will do so in the future? I ask, to what does experience extend? We have had experience of past events. As what was once future has gradually become the present, we have seen events, which once were future, repeat themselves. But how can this justify us in arriving at the conclusion that nature is uniform, and that they must continue to do so? Our belief that they will do so is an inference, and cannot therefore be founded on experience alone. Some principle, distinct from it, must exist in the mind, which justifies us in arriving at this conclusion.

28. Nor can it be arrived at by any process of deductive reasoning. No premiss can be found, resting on any self-evident principle, which can justify the conclusion that the uture must, under similar conditions, resemble the past.

29. Let us recur to the example, that the sun will rise to-morrow. How do we know this? The answer which this philosophy gives, is that we believe it, because we have had experience that it has always done so; and that our experience has reached to the point that what was once future has become past. But this can say nothing as to a future which has not yet become past. Now, it is both conceivable and possible, despite of any amount of past experience, that the sun may not rise again to-morrow; or, to put the same truth in general terms, that the blind forces of nature may suddenly or gradually cease to repeat themselves.

30. If the first man who saw the sun rise had been in full possession of his reasoning powers, it is evident that from seeing it rise once, he could have drawn no inference as to what it

would do in future. All he could have done would have been to draw the conclusion that it might rise again. Nor would two or three repetitions have justified the conclusion that it would do so. But a large number of such repetitions—it is impossible to say how many—would generate the feeling of certainty. How comes this? The only possible explanation is, that there is some principle in our mental constitution which compels us to arrive at this conclusion, and that it cannot be given by experience alone. The device of referring it to a number of experiences of our remote ancestors, which may have generated an intuitive belief in us, their descendants, as an account of its origin, only removes the difficulty without attempting to solve it. The necessity of explaining what gave validity to the original experience remains in full force. Similar reasoning applies to every axiomatic principle, and to all certainties which lie at the foundation of all valid reasoning.

31. All proof must rest on something which does not require proof. Premisses cannot run up into infinity. To assert that everything must be proved is to deny the possibility of reasoning. Some premisses are acquiesced in owing to their self-evidence, or to something in our mental constitution which compels us to assent to them. They must therefore possess an universal objective validity, independent of our experience of phenomena, however closely they may be connected with it. It is unnecessary to determine whether these principles are few or many : it is sufficient that they exist. Their existence destroys the basis on which the philosophy of pantheism and atheism rests.

32. We must now consider another most important principle on which this philosophy is founded, viz., its denial that the order and adaptations of nature are a sufficient ground for inferring the existence of an intelligent and conscious mind, which the philosophy of theism designates as a Personal God. The affirmation of certain systems of current philosophy is clear, and leaves no doubtful issue, viz., that we are not justified from the presence of order in nature in inferring the existence of an arranger; or from adaptation, of an adapter, or from apparent contrivance, of a contriver; or from the suitableness of the means by which a definite result has been brought about to effectuate it, of a designer. In one word, it is affirmed, when we see in nature results which elsewhere are unquestionable evidences of the presence of intelligent mind, that all such inferences are invalid in the domains of nature; and that in making them we are only transferring the subjective impressions of our own minds into objective facts. On the contrary, this philosophy teaches that the order and adapta-

tions of nature are not due to the presence of conscious intelligence; but of latent unintelligent self-evolution. To put the matter broadly: it is affirmed that intelligence has not produced nature, its order and adaptations, but that nature is the storehouse from which unintelligent law and latent forces have evolved all these wonderful phenomena. Non-life has generated life; unintelligence, intelligence; unconsciousness, self-consciousness; impersonality, personality; necessary law, freedom; latent forces, moral agents. One aspect of pantheistic philosophy postulates the presence of unconscious intelligence in nature. But what is its nature, how it acts, or in what it is inherent, it leaves involved in a haziness which far exceeds that of any mystery involved in theism.

33. Let us do these theories justice. It is affirmed that our conceptions of order and adaptation are essentially human, and have no validity when they are applied to anything which is not the product of the human mind. Also it is affirmed, that all analogy fails between the works of nature and those of man; and that this renders invalid the conclusions which the theist seeks to draw from them.

34. I reply, that the objection is invalid, because, if true, it condemns us to universal ignorance. Our conceptions of law, force, and energy, are human conceptions, the creation of our own minds. If this is a reason why they must be invalid in the one case, it is no less so why our reasonings respecting them must be invalid in the other. The objection is suicidal, and one which would render all philosophy impossible.

35. But further: when we contemplate order and adaptation, we do not infer from it the presence of any particular form of intelligence, but of intelligence generally; just as when we speak of matter, time, and place, we do not confine them to the special subjects from which we have derived our conception of them; but we apply them to phenomena generally. It is perfectly true that within the range of our experience, men and animals are the only beings who are capable of producing the results of order and adaptation. We have evidence that among these, different orders of intelligence exist. We are therefore justified in concluding that different orders and degrees of intelligence may exist in regions beyond our experience; though they may differ in some respects from that of men.

36. I admit that there are a few cases in which order and adaptation have resulted from the action of that which, for want of a better term, we designate chance. Such, however, are so rare, and the instances so imperfect, that they are not worthy of consideration in the present argument. One thing is certain. As far as our experience goes, chance is only

capable of producing such results on a very diminutive scale, and after long intervals of time. Yet, the principle of chance is largely invoked in aid of the theories of this philosophy ; though all experience affirms that it is incapable of producing the results in question.

37. The all-important fact to be observed is that, as far as experience goes, lucky chances have no tendency to repeat themselves. On the contrary, the occurrence of one once is a reason why we should expect it not to occur again. Whenever such a result takes place frequently, we cannot help inferring that this must be due to the intervention of mind. Let us take an example. If we were to throw up twelve dice into the air at hap-hazard, it is possible, though in the highest degree improbable, that they might all fall with their aces uppermost. But if the operation were repeated one hundred times, and the same result followed, there is no one who is capable of understanding the operation who would not draw the conclusion that the dice were heavily loaded as the highest of certitudes. The case is precisely similar with respect to the order and adaptations of nature. They are not only numerous but innumerable. It follows, therefore, that nature in every part is loaded heavily, and that that which loads it is the Divine mind.*

---

* I am quite aware if twelve dice should fall with their aces uppermost, that, mathematically speaking, it is quite as probable that they would do so a second time, supposing the operation to be repeated under precisely similar conditions. Just in the same way, if a person held twenty bonds in a foreign loan, of which there were annual drawings, if one of these should be drawn, the chance that one or all of the remaining nineteen would be drawn at any subsequent year would be equally good, and would be entirely unaffected by the drawing of the twentieth. This, however, in no way affects my argument, which is founded entirely on experience and fact. There can be no doubt that if twelve dice were thrown up into the air, and they fell one hundred times in succession with their aces uppermost, every one possessed of common sense would consider it the greatest of certitudes that foul play had been had recourse to ; or in other words, he would attribute the result, not to the action of blind forces or laws, but to the presence of intelligence. The same remark is true respecting the bonds. If a particular bondholder were to draw a prize at every drawing, and others never, the inference would be arrived at, that the whole matter was managed dishonestly, and had resulted, not from the action of blind forces acting according to invariable laws, but from fraudulent intelligence. In a similar manner, when order and adaptation are the result of the action of natural forces, and are brought about by these forces intersecting one another at the right time and place, the inference is no less certain, that such results cannot be due to the action of a number of blind forces, but to intelligence. Those against whom I am reasoning profess to found their philosophy on an ultimate basis of fact and experience. I reply to it by a conclusive appeal to the same principle.

38. It will be objected that this philosophy nowhere affirms that order and adaptation have been evolved by chance action, but by forces working in conformity with immutable law. I reply that chance is only another name for the blind action of unintelligent laws and forces, and that the only additional factor introduced by the term chance is, that two or more of these forces or laws happen to intersect one another at a time and place suitable for producing a particular result, and without which concurrence the result could not have existed. When these do so at such a time and place, that a particular effect is the result of their intersection, this is what we call a lucky chance. What I mean will be more easily understood by an illustration. Let us suppose a rock undergoing the process of disintegration. The action of water and of frost has opened in it several fissures. In accordance with another set of natural laws, the wind, or some other force, carries into them at this particular moment a number of seeds. These take root; fresh disintegration takes place. The operation is repeated; and thus the process is accelerated far more than it could have been by the action of a single force. This philosophy is compelled to invoke the aid of such lucky concurrences of forces in numbers numberless. Without them it would be powerless to impart to its speculations even the appearance of probability. In addition to this, it demands the right of drawing to any extent on the eternity of the past for an indefinite amount of time for the purpose of carrying on its operations. What is not possible in one hundred years may happen in one million. In this manner, with the bank of of eternity at command, all things are possible.

39. I submit that this mode of reasoning is not to solve the question, but to evade it. It gives no real account of the origin of those adaptations with which the universe abounds. On the contrary, there is something in the constitution of our minds which compels us when we contemplate an adaptation of complicated parts, exactly fitted to produce a suitable result, and observe that the result is brought about by the adaptation, to infer that it has been effected by the action of intelligence. Reason arrives at the conclusion that order and adaptation cannot have resulted from the action of unintelligent forces, but of intelligent mind. This will be the invariable inference, except where the exigencies of a particular theory compel those who hold it to renounce the convictions of common sense. Let it be observed that I am speaking, not of some imperfect condition of the human savage, but of the fully developed intellect of cultivated men.

40. The importance of this principle in reference to the philosophy of Pantheism and Atheism is strikingly brought before us in the celebrated work of Strauss, entitled *The Old Faith and the New*, in which he professes not simply to state his own opinions, but to be acting as the mouthpiece of a large number of German unbelievers. As this work has already gone through more than one edition in our language, besides the large number that it had previously gone through in Germany, it will be necessary to give it a special attention, for the purpose of exposing the unsound basis of its philosophy. The questions discussed in it are such that it is impossible to exaggerate their importance. They are as follows: In answer to the question, Are we still Christians? in the name of advanced thought in Germany, he answers in the negative. In reply to the question, Have we a religion? the answer is of a similar import. In answer to the question, What is our conception of the universe? his reply assumes the form of a material Pantheism, which differs in nothing from Atheism except in an illicit use of the language of Theism. Lastly, wonderful to say, in answer to the question, What is our rule of life? he announces himself a thorough-going German conservative, and utters a loud protest against the various forms of Communistic Atheism. It would appear that he and those in whose name he speaks are of opinion that the only effective mode to bar out the ocean is to demolish the old strongly-built sea-wall to its foundations, which has for ages past successfully repelled its billows, and in future to attempt to dam them out by substituting for it a thin layer of sand.

41. The faith into which the author's philosophy has conducted him, and those in whose name he speaks, is that of the existence of a Cosmos, the sum total of all being, material, mental, and moral, including all existence and its laws, but which is void of personality, which is deaf to the voice of prayer; in which the place of volition is supplied by necessary and unyielding laws; of an intelligent Creator, by a self-developing power utterly unconscious, which to man is incapable of being the object of either hope or trust; which in the course of its self-development has evolved both the individual and the race, and will crush them again beneath the heel of iron destiny. This power will, through the endless whirl of the eternities of time and the infinities of space, go on evolving fresh worlds out of the ashes of preceding ones, and endless successions of systems and of galaxies, in which we as individuals shall take no part, to be again absorbed into the bosom of the mighty infinite. At death our self-conscious existence shall perish, never to be renewed. The atoms which compose us, after having been absorbed into

the unconscious infinite, may be useful as materials for future life : but the hope and the destiny of the individual is eternal silence. To this, the only alleviation which this philosophy affords, is the consideration that while our conscious selves have utterly perished, the cosmos will go on evolving fresh forms of life and beauty throughout eternity, and will crush them again beneath the iron wheels of its chariot. No feeling of responsibility for the past need disturb us. Our destiny is non-entity.

42. Such is the general sum total—the net result which this philosophy propounds to us in lieu of Theism. A few quotations from it will place its principles in a striking light.

43. "The argument of the old religion was, that as the reasonable and the good in mankind proceed from conscious-ness and will, that, therefore, which on a large scale corresponds to this in the world must likewise proceed from an Author endowed with intelligent volition. We have given up this mode of inference. We no longer regard the Cosmos as the work of a reasonable and good Creator, but rather as the laboratory of the reasonable and good. We consider it not as planned by the highest reason, but planned for the highest reason. The Cosmos is simultaneously both cause and effect, the outward and the inward together." Again, "We stand here at the limits of our knowledge. We gaze into the abyss, we can fathom no further. But this, at least, is certain, that the personal image which meets our gaze there is but the reflection of the wondering spectator himself. If we always bear this in mind, there would be as little objection to the expression 'God' as to that of the rising and setting of the sun, when we are all the time conscious of the actual circumstances." After these and numerous similar assertions, the following utterance is remarkable : "At any rate, that in which we feel ourselves entirely dependent is by no means merely a rude power, to which we bow in mute resignation; but is at the same time both order and law, reason and goodness, to which we surrender ourselves in loving trust. More than this, as we perceive in ourselves the same disposition to the reasonable and the good, which we recognize in the Cosmos; and find ourselves to be beings by whom it is felt and recognized, in whom it is to become personified; we also feel ourselves related in our inmost nature to that on which we are dependent; we discover ourselves at the same time to be free in that dependence, and pride and humility, joy and submission intermingle in the feeling for the Cosmos."

44. Such is the substitute which this philosophy provides for

(9)　　　　　　c

a personal God. We are to feel all this for a being (if an infinite Cosmos can be called a being) who has neither personality, intelligence, nor will, who is the prey of inexorable law, who is incapable alike of affection and of thought; who, if he has children, has not made a single provision for their wants, cares not for them, and in due time inexorably devours them. Surely the theories of Atheism are rational compared with a Pantheism, which offers such adulation to a Cosmos which can neither see, hear, feel, nor think, which is alike incapable of affections and intelligent volition. Truly, one is reminded of the mocking of Elijah, "Cry aloud, for he is a god. Surely he sleepeth, and must be awaked."

45. One of the atheistic friends of our author, whose works he advises the reader not to glance at but to study, pronounces that it would have been better if the universe had never existed; and if no life had ever arisen in the earth any more than in the moon. This assertion is certainly not invalidated by Strauss's thin logic. "If it be true," says he, "it follows that the thought that it would have been better if the universe had never existed, had better not to have existed likewise." One can hardly help thinking that the following passage must have been written in irony.

46. "Sallies of this kind, as we remarked, impress our intelligence as absurd, but our feelings as blasphemous. We consider it arrogant and profane on the part of a single individual to oppose himself with such audacious levity to the Cosmos whence he springs, from which also he derives that spark of reason which he misuses."

47. But I must now draw attention to some of the principles from which the author considers that these are natural conclusions.

48. He begins with the conception of the Cosmos, which he defines "not only as the sum total of all phenomena, but also of all forces and of all laws. The All," says he, "being the All; nothing can exist outside it; it seems even to include the void beyond." After having pointed out the various changes through which its various parts have passed, he goes on to assert that this infinite Cosmos constitutes a unity. "The Cosmos itself," says he, "the sum total of infinite worlds, in all stages of growth and decay, abides eternally unchanged in the constancy of its absolute energy amidst the everlasting revolution and mutation of its parts."

49. I have quoted these passages for the purpose of showing that the fundamental difficulties of this philosophy fully equal those of theism, against which it is in vain for it to urge that it enters into the regions of the unknowable. If the universe is

the sum total of all phenomena, forces, and laws, a few questions may be propounded for its solution. Is it nothing but these? Are phenomena and laws possessed of an objective existence, or must something else underlie them? Are laws existences, or modes of existence, or what are they? Are its forces actually existent things, or qualities inherent in them? Again, "the Cosmos is the sum total of infinite worlds." It is therefore infinite, but consists of finite parts. Can it therefore be a unity? It follows, then, that that which is infinite is not absolutely unthinkable, and that some of the conceptions which are derived from our finite modes of being may be projected into it without violating any principle of sound philosophy. But further, this infinite universe consists of parts several of which are infinite; it follows, therefore, that an infinitude which is composed of subordinate infinities, can constitute a unity. But, as a crowning mystery, we are told that it abides eternally unchanged in the constancy of its absolute energy amidst the everlasting revolution and mutation of its parts. Surely a philosophy which admits a number of such positions among its fundamental principles may be asked to show a little modesty when it assails the difficulties of theism. The one contains unfathomable mysteries equally as the other.

50. But, says our author, "the Cosmos is a phœnix, ever recovering itself from its ashes." Yes, surely, it is a consolatory truth for men who will never renew their personal existence to be assured that their remorseless parent never had a beginning to its activities, and never shall have an end, but that it shall continue throughout the infinities of time and space to cast up the bubbles of phenomena, and devour them, to reappear again in endless progression. Yet this is the god of this philosophy, who goes on endlessly reproducing himself, under the impulse of blind forces directed by equally blind laws, in endless forms of life and death, of reproduction and decay, throughout the dismal eternity of the future. Full well may Strauss's Atheist friend satirize the folly of such a god. But, no: he is alike incapable of wisdom and of folly; though he contains in himself potentiality, and evolves into actuality all wisdom and all folly, all order and disorder, all growth and decay, all good and evil, all virtue and all crime. Verily, such a god cannot be a phœnix, but a Proteus. Yet our author, and those in whose name he speaks, assert that they think it worthy of a reverent regard, and that to insult it is a blasphemy!

51. There is an obvious difficulty which confronts this philosophy, of which it does not attempt to offer a solution. If the Cosmos is thus eternally reproductive, why may it not at some

period during the infinity of future time reproduce our own personal existence, and even hold us responsible for what we have done in our previous state of being? To do so would only be to add one wonder more to the multitude of wonders which it is declared to be able to effect. Against this most serious contingency this philosophy has nothing to offer, but its dogmatic assertion that personal existence, after its fleeting phenomenal appearance, must sink into eternal silence.

52. Let us now examine some of the processes by which it attempts to account for the origin of the existing order of things. With respect to some of the processes by means of which it affirms the universe of matter to have been constructed, we need have no difficulty. They may have been the very means which the Creator has employed to effectuate His purposes; and to accept them as denoting the law according to which creation has been evolved is quite consistent with a belief in Theism. As all His manifestations with which we are acquainted are in conformity with law, and involve the use of means, so there is no difficulty in conceiving that God's creative work has been conducted in conformity with a definite law and order, and that He has made use of means in effecting it, instead of creating each separate existence immediately. On the contrary, it is highly probable that such would be the mode of His action.

53. But this is widely different from the assumption that the Cosmos can have been built up by the action of blind forces without the aid of intelligence and will. Law, however convenient as a term, denotes nothing but an invariable mode of action. In itself it embraces no conception of energy or power, although nothing is more common even in philosophic language than to confound this conception with it. But it is impossible to build the universe without the energetic action of both these. Unless forces have an action given to them, they can effect nothing,—confusion, not harmonious arrangement, will be the results of their operations. These can only be found in intelligence and will. As far as human experience extends, forces acting in conformity with blind laws, have never produced a single adaptation, order, or arrangement, but destruction only. This philosophy, for the purpose of enabling it to dispense with the directing power of intelligence and will, postulates an eternity of time, during which forces have acted, and affirms that this can produce all the results of intelligent volition.

54. Having evolved the matter of the universe into planets, suns, and systems, by means which the Theist need not dispute, as long as they have an omnipotent intelligence at their back,

energizing in and through them, our author is compelled to face the question of the origin of life. He is fully aware of the difficulty of the problem, and admits that it is no solution of it to say, that its absence may be accounted for in the lower strata, by the supposition that causes may have been in existence, which have destroyed all traces of it. "There was a time," says he, "when the temperature of the earth was so high, that living organisms could not exist on it. There was once no organic life on the earth: at a later period there was: it must consequently have had a beginning, and the question is how?"

55. Yes, truly; that is the question. Kant judged that it might well be said, "Give me matter, and I will explain the origin of the world; but not, Give me matter, and I will explain the origin of a caterpillar." Let it not be forgotten also that Kant bowed in reverence before the moral nature of man, and its authoritative affirmation of the obligation of the moral law. These mighty gulfs, however, the philosophy of Atheism and Pantheism has attempted to bridge over. "Here," says Strauss, "faith intervenes with its miracle." This philosophy postulates an operation no less miraculous, viz., the action of blind forces under the direction of blind laws, continued throughout an eternity of time.

56. I need hardly say, that our author resolves all difficulties by boldly assuming the truth of the theory of spontaneous generation. Here let it be observed, that Atheism is obliged to use a word, which implies the presence of will. He admits the uncertainty of previous experiments; but nothing daunted, he affirms, "If the question of spontaneous generation could not be proved in regard to our present terrestrial period, this would establish nothing with respect to a primeval period under totally different conditions. The existence of the crudest form of life has however never been actually demonstrated. Life too, after all, is nothing but a form of motion."

57. On questions of pure physics I shall not enter. But it belongs to the present inquiry to point out the conditions of the problem which this philosophy has to solve; and not to allow it to substitute an unreal for the true issue. That issue is not the one here stated. Before it can advance one step, proof positive of the truth of the theory of spontaneous generation must be given. It is no solution of the problem, to take refuge in the assumed possibility, that it may have taken place under widely different conditions during the uncertain past. To do so is cunningly to assume the question at issue. Professor Huxley tells us that proof of the theory of spontaneous generation has yet to be given.

58. But further: supposing a living being of the lowest type could be constructed in the laboratory, does this bring us one atom nearer to the point at issue? The real question is, whence comes living matter? and what is the distinction between it and non-living matter? There our opponents, being the judges, differ *toto cœlo* from each other. Is there any evidence that matter which has never lived, can be made to pass into living forms? Till this can be shown, the mere formation of a being in the laboratory, which possesses the lowest form of life, proves nothing. The only adequate solution of this question on the pantheistic and atheistic side is proof positive that life is a mode of motion, and nothing else. This proof has certainly not yet been adduced, and even if it could be found, there is yet a further question which demands an answer; viz. how, whence, and where has originated this peculiar modification of motion which constitutes life; and how has it come into existence at the favourable moment for its existence? Had it not been favourable, the feeble germ would have been crushed by the mighty powers of nature in the struggle for existence. All this and much more must be answered before it can be proved, that mechanical or chemical forces can become vital ones by any powers which they possess of self-transmutation.

59. Our author endeavours to evade the question by concealing it behind a mass of scientific jargon. He says:— "Life is only a special, viz. the most complicated, form of mechanics. A part of the sum total of matter emerges from time to time out of the usual course of its motions into special thermico-organic combinations; and after having for a time continued therein, it returns again to the general modes of motion."

60. When we are famishing for scientific bread, it is cruel for philosophy to throw us a stone. As an account of the matter we are considering, part of the above sentence is unintelligible, and the remainder attempts to answer one difficulty by raising others far greater.

61. The perusal of this work affords a striking proof that the philosophers in whose names it is written were far from being satisfied with their position, even after they had obtained possession of an inorganic cell, from whence they might commence the operation of creating the various forms of organic life, of which man is the crown. They felt deeply, in the words of our author, "that no acorn ever produces a fig; that a fish always produces a fish, and never a bird or a reptile; a sheep always produces a sheep, and never a bull or a goat."

They have therefore hailed, as the rising of a new sun, the theory of natural selection as a means for constructing the worlds of life and organism, without the intervention of a Creator. For the use they make of it it is possible that its author will owe them little thanks; but they are almost ready to forgive Mr. Darwin for his postulate of the original intervention of a God to infuse into inorganic matter the principle of life, in consideration of the greatness of his discovery. He is with them, the founder of the new age, in which the belief in the being of a God is destined to become an old wife's fable.

62. Let it be observed, however, that the Darwinian theory, whatever be its merits or defects, is only a special form of a theory of creation by evolution. It assumes, in the first instance, a creative act, by which some cells had infused into them the principle of life. It then proceeds to account for the existence of every living form by the aid of two principles, designated natural and sexual selection, without any subsequent intervention of Divine power. Whatever may be thought of this particular theory, it is evident that a principle of evolution, by which I mean that all existing organisms have been gradually evolved from one another by the Creator's wisdom and power, through certain forces of which He possesses the absolute control, is as consistent with Theism as any other theory of creation. The only theories which are essentially atheistic and pantheistic are those which lay down that God is not the author of the laws of nature, nor their contriver, nor the director of their operations, and that blind forces can produce the phenomena which result from the operation of intelligence, and that forces can exist independently of His constant energy. The old theory of creation was, that each species was produced by a separate creative act, the idea being that its progenitors must have started into being entire and complete. This may or may not have been the *modus operandi* employed by the Creator; but, as a theory, it leaves us in the dark how creation was effected, except that it was the result of the exertion of the divine will. A theory of development professes to give the law of progress and to account for some of the means through which creation has been accomplished. Whether it has been effected in this way, or in that, can only be determined by the facts of nature which throw light on the subject. To speak of creation out of nothing as an adequate solution of how creation has been effected is only a confession of our ignorance. The real point is, is the theory suggested an adequate account of the facts of nature? Are the means

adequate to produce the result? Or must other agencies have contributed to it, and among them the direct intervention of God?

63. There is, unquestionably, a tendency among religious men to charge every theory of creation by evolution with pantheistic and atheistic tendencies. This would be just, if it were a necessary part of such theories, that blind forces and laws are able to produce this result independently of the power and intelligence of a personal God. But where I ask, is the Pantheism and Atheism, if we assume that the Creator has followed a definite order and law in His creative acts, and has carried them on, as He does all the acts of His providence, by the use of means? Or if, instead of causing the first progenitors of a species to spring up from the ground, He has produced them out of beings previously in existence? Our present knowledge is very inadequate to determine how creation has been effected. This is a strong reason why we should avoid prematurely dogmatizing; but, certainly, none why we should not make it the subject of careful study.

64. There are not wanting indications that in the formation of the universe the Creator has acted through the agency of means, and not by that which we designate direct action. Of this the evidence is considerable. Whether this be an entire account of the matter is quite another question. Still more clear is it that His creative acts have followed a sequence and order, and been constituted on a general plan. This latter point must be admitted even by those who refuse to admit the theory of creation by evolution. We might have hoped that the general acquiescence in the well-known illustration of Paley's watch, would have been a sufficient safeguard against wholesale denunciations of those who hold this theory as if it were destructive of Theism. As he observes, if a watch could be so constructed as to produce another watch by its mechanism, and should thus go on producing a succession of watches, each possessed of the power of self-reparation, we should feel the most profound admiration for the skill of the artist. Nor would it be diminished, if the mechanism could construct a first-rate chronometer; and this a succession of still more perfect instruments. The only point in which such a theory can be either pantheistic or atheistic is when it is assumed that such harmonics can have resulted from the action of blind forces, without the intervention of intelligence.

65. Still more remarkable is it that such a theory should be suspected of pantheistic or atheistic tendencies, when we reflect that the mode in which God has created every individual

is by a process of evolution. Yet, surely, it will not be pre-
tended that He has not made each one of us, and every individual of every species. Yet He has unquestionably effected
this by a process of evolution. The media through which He
works may be very obscure; but this does not affect the fact
itself. History also teaches that in man the evolution of more
perfect from less perfect states, is the order of God's providen-
tial government of the world. The New Testament declares
that revelation has been communicated in a similar manner.
Why, then, may not the Creator have created different species
by producing one out of another by a process unknown to us.
It is absurd to attempt to shut up all inquiries on this subject,
by asserting that all such theories are either pantheistic or
atheistic.

66. Still, it is undeniable that the Darwinian form of this
theory has been widely embraced by the philosophic schools in
question, as affording an apparent solution of some of their
difficulties. The joy with which they have hailed its advent is
very remarkable. It becomes, therefore, a duty thoroughly to
examine into its ability to produce the results in question, and
to estimate the difficulties with which it is attended. Yet, it
must not be forgotten that its author distinctly assumes the
necessity of a Creator to infuse into matter the first forms of
life, and to impress on it its laws. This difficulty can only be
got over by Pantheists and Atheists by the exercise of a hearty
faith in some unknown powers of the past or discoveries of the
future. It follows, therefore, that the faith which they deride
in connection with religion and Christianity is essential to this
philosophy. It demands the exercise of faith in the unseen, viz.,
the discoveries of the future or the unknown possibilities of the
past, for without it it is destitute of even the semblance of proof.
It would seem as if faith in the unseen is only objectionable
when it is demanded in connection with religion.

67. It follows, therefore, that it is impossible for these
systems to bridge over the interval which separates life from
not-life. There is also another interval which can be spanned by
no arch, viz., the production of the power of sensation. According to these theories, there must have been a time when there
was no sensation in that part of the universe to which we
belong. There, therefore, must have been a time when the
first being which was capable of sensation sprang into existence.
Pantheism will, perhaps, affirm that the infinite Cosmos has
ever possessed within itself sensation and intelligence. If so,
particles capable of sensation must have existed in that fire
mist out of which the present order of things has been evolved,

the heat of which was sufficient to have sustained all existing matter in the form of gas. If so, their existence must have been very uncomfortable during the countless ages the matter of the solar and sidereal systems has taken in cooling. The alternative will doubtless be preferred, that a time once was, when the first being capable of sensation began to be. But a vast interval separates the sentient from the non-sentient, not a succession of trifling variations. The philosophy which attempts to construct a universe without the intervention of a God is bound to give us an account of how the first sentient being began to be.

68. But there are several other states of being which are separated from each other, not by short steps but by vast intervals. Among these self-consciousness occupies a conspicuous place. It is obvious that it exists. It is as certain as any fact of time or space. We can all and each of us utter the mysterious word "I," and attach a distinct meaning to it. It is the most mysterious of words. Who shall fathom its profound depths? It is that which separates between self and not-self, person and thing. It is that which constitutes us a unity in the midst of plurality and change. As beings capable of self-consciousness, we feel that we have existed through long intervals of time, surrounded by and deeply interested in multitudes of things which are not ourselves. Not one particle of matter constitutes our present bodies which composed them twenty years since, yet we are the same. There must have been a time when self-conscious beings existed not. There must, therefore, have been one when a self-conscious being first began to be. Here then is an interval the depth of which the imagination can but imperfectly fathom. It is not too much to say, that no theory of evolution can bridge this over without the intervention of a self-conscious Creator.

69. There is yet another interval. A being may be a person, and yet have no conception of right or duty. I select this conception as representative of the whole moral nature of man, of which it forms the most remarkable characteristic. It is immaterial to my argument whether the utilitarian philosophy is correct in its analysis of the origin of the idea. I firmly believe that it is not. But the fact cannot be gainsaid, that vast numbers of minds, of the highest order, have a clear conception of duty quite distinct from any reference to utilitarianism. On the contrary, they feel the strongest obligation to sacrifice themselves to it in contradiction to the strongest dictates of expediency. There is something within us which says, let right prevail, even if the heavens fall. There must, therefore, have

been a time when the first being, who was capable of feeling a sense of duty, who could bow before a moral law, and say, "I ought," began to be. The interval is one which separates the conception of duty from non-duty; of conscience from non-conscience; of a moral nature from the want of it. The difference is not one of degree but of kind. Between laws of motion and their modifications, and conceptions of duty, there is no one thing in common. When the idea of duty first originated a new order of being entered the universe.

70. Even if the principle of the utilitarian philosophy is correct, that duty is the obligation to seek the greatest happiness of the greatest number, the argument is unaffected by it. The question still imperatively demands solution, how came it ever to be felt to be a duty, to seek the greatest happiness of the greatest number? When and how has this sentiment arisen? Of what form of motion is it the modification?

71. Such are some of the gaps which must be bridged over by means of clear and indisputable facts, before a philosophy which has no other forces at its command but blind, unintelligent ones, can account for the origin of things. But supposing for argument's sake that these have been surmounted, the question at once arises, whether the pantheistic and atheistic theory of evolution is adequate to account for the existence of the various orders of beings which lie within these bounds. I will now examine some of the special agencies by which it has been attempted to be shown that the various forms of organized life have been developed without the agency of a being possessed of personal intelligence and power. The only principles which this philosophy presses into its service for that purpose are Darwin's two principles of natural and sexual selection.

72. I by no means wish to affirm that these may not have been potent instruments in the hands of Omnipotence by which God has carried on His creative work. That they act within certain limits is an obvious fact. The question is, what are those limits? Are they the only agencies? Are they alone adequate to the work? Must not other principles, known and unknown, have contributed to it? Is their distinct and separate agency conceivable without Omnipotence at their back?

73. We must begin by assuming that life has somehow originated in the earth. The problem before us is as follows: given matter and force acting in conformity with invariable laws, both alike destitute of intelligence, to evolve everything in the sentient universe, which bears the indications of the action of intelligence. Let us even suppose that one or more cells have been evolved from which our course of evolution is to com-

mence which is ultimately to culminate in the production of man.

74. There is one resource to which this philosophy flies in every difficulty, and which it uses with unbounded freedom,—an infinite storehouse of past time. If a thing cannot be effected in one thousand years, it can in a million; if not in a million, it can in one hundred million. If the last period is inadequate, boldly multiply, for it is impossible to break the bank of the eternity of the past. With this agency at its command, all things are possible. Let us hear Strauss :—" Short steps and longest intervals of time are the magic formula by which actual science at present solves the mystery of the universe: they are the talismans by whose aid she quite naturally unlocks the portals, formerly reputed to fly asunder at the sole bidding of miracle."

75. Yes, truly : there is more truth in this passage than its author probably intended to convey. The action of this principle is truly magical and talismanic; it is worthy of the deep consideration of those who invoke it, whether it can effect any results more real than the magical formularies and talismans of the *Arabian Nights*. Little jumps, and infinite time to jump in, is all that is required to evolve all the order and adaptations of the universe, which exist in numbers passing all comprehension. The proposition that, if we have time enough to walk to a galaxy, compared with which the distance of Sirius is a speck, by taking steps of an inch long, we shall get there in the course of infinite time, may be incapable of being disproved ; but it is absurd. I submit that this continual invocation of infinite time is not a rational solution of a difficulty, but an evasion of it.

76. The truth is that physical science breaks this magic wand in the hands of the operator. While it tells us that the universe has existed a vast interval of time in its present form, it affirms that it cannot have existed for an indefinite one. The laws of its physical forces assign to it clear and definite limits, which it cannot have exceeded. It follows, therefore, that indefinite demands on a past eternity cannot be tolerated by a sound philosophy.

77. Not only is this philosophy compelled to assume that a number of small variations must have taken place, which for any practical purpose it is impossible to distinguish from infinite; but it is compelled to take for granted that all those have been on the side of progressive improvement. Yet the history of man testifies that nature has made many failures and retrogressions. Human progress has been, unhappily,

full of them. But these are easily got rid of by the theory of the destruction of the weakest and the survival of the strongest in the struggle for existence. Yet history informs us that some of the weak races of mankind have a remarkable tenacity of life.

78. But if such a tendency exists in nature, this philosophy is bound to give us some account of its origin. Tendencies in nature on the side of progress are very useful ones. It is, therefore, a serious question, How got they there? For ought that appears, blind matter, force, and law might have produced tendencies suited to shiver systems to pieces, and not to construct them. Does not the existence of such tendencies imply the presence of superintending mind?

79. But, says this philosophy, all that is necessary is to continue advancing by slow and gradual variations; and this glorious universe, with all its complicated adaptations, crowned by man, will appear at last! We need not care for the shortness nor the variety of the steps, nor for occasional movements in a backward direction; for have we not infinite time at our command? The cell, with its lowest forms of life, or the intellectual or moral atoms diffused in yonder fire-mist, will in due time produce all the complicated organisms of living beings, with their wondrous adaptations, and at length a Newton, a Shakespeare, and a self-denying Howard.

80. But, I ask emphatically, are such short steps all that is required? Shall we not be brought to a standstill by the absence of necessary conditions? Blind forces cannot effect their work except by the aid of things which, for want of a better name, we must call favourable chances, by which I mean forces intersecting one another at the right time and place. What myriads of forces must have worked in vain for the want of this condition of successful operation? Let me illustrate this by the example which Strauss has chosen as an illustration of the manner in which we may readily account for the production of the various organisms of nature. "Let us suppose," says he, " a herd of cattle in primitive times to be still destitute of horns, only possessed of powerful necks and projecting foreheads. The herd is attacked by beasts of prey: it defends itself by running against them and butting with the head. The butting will be the more vigorous, the bulls the fitter to resist the beasts of prey, the harder the forehead with which he butts. Should this butting in an individual have developed into an incipient horny accretion, then such an individual would have the best chance of preserving his existence. If the less equipped bulls of such a herd were torn to pieces, then the

individual thus equipped would propagate the species. Unquestionably there would be some at least among its descendants in whose case the paternal equipment would be repeated; and if on renewed attacks these very ones again survived, and, moreover, principally those whose horns were most developed, then little by little, by transmission of this weapon to the other sex, a completely horned species would be formed, especially if the other sex would of its accord give the preference to the males thus ornamented; and here Darwin's theory of natural selection is supplemented by the so-called sexual selection, to which he has recently devoted a special work."

81. Few of the operations of nature would seem to be more simple than the manufacture of a horn; let us, therefore, carefully examine the amount of time and lucky chance which this theory finds it necessary to postulate as necessary for its formation. This will give us a clear idea of the difficulties which must have been surmounted in the course of the evolution of man from an inorganic cell, if there was nothing but unintelligent forces to operate with.

I. The theory before us presupposes a very favourable concurrence of circumstances with which to commence our operations. Nature has already kindly furnished us with a herd of cattle, with powerful necks and protruding foreheads. How long it must have taken to form these latter appendages this philosophy does not tell us. Having eternity at its command, it simply brandishes its magic wand and says, as indefinite a number of eons of past time as you require.

II. Another favourable condition is provided all ready for our use. It seems that a horn cannot be grown on a hornless animal without the exercise of butting; accordingly, a number of beasts of prey are at hand at the proper time and place to offer battle to our unhorned herd—these, be it observed, are supposed to be fully equipped with all their weapons of offence. But suppose that these latter had come into existence at a different time and place, or that instead of our oxen being surrounded by beasts of prey, they had come into existence among a number of peaceful creatures, the whole operation of horn-growing must have come to a standstill. The concurrence of such favourable contingencies could only have occurred after the lapse of indefinite eons.

III. The herd, when attacked, defend themselves by butting. It was fortunate that nature should have furnished them with this impulse. This looks like the presence of intelligence, for unintelligent nature might quite as well have provided them with a disposition to run away when attacked, as she has the hare, and there would have been no tendency to generate a 'horn. Such a disposition must have required the concurrence of multitudes of favourable circumstances for its formation, as well as that of indefinite eons of time.

IV. The act of butting has a tendency to harden the skull; this we know to be a fact. Still, a philosophy whose object is not theory, but truth, cannot help inquiring, Whence came this tendency? It might have been one in an opposite direction.

V. We are next invited to assume that repeated acts of butting have not only hardened the skull, but developed a horny accretion. The remarks of our author might lead the reader to believe that all this could have been effected in a single generation of bull life. But it is quite evident that it could only have been the result of the struggles of protracted generations, who succeeded in transmitting to their descendants a gradually increasing horny appendage. If it were not so, bull life in those primeval ages must have been protracted to a period compared with which the age of Methuselah must have been as nothing. Let it be observed also, that the concurrence of every one of these favourable conditions must have been continually repeating themselves.

VI. The bulls, says our author, who have succeeded in developing these horny appendages will have the best chance of preserving their existence. Still this is a chance only, but not a certainty, for many other contingencies might have destroyed them. Deaths from disease were probably not unknown in primeval times, and against this the possession of an incipient horn would have been no prevention.

VII. We are next asked to assume that these bulls go on continually fighting until all the less-equipped ones are torn in pieces, in order that an individual with incipient horns may become the progenitor of a race. This philosophy, however, is utterly silent as to the number of years and of favourable contingencies it would have taken to bring about this result. It simply brandishes its magic wand, and the unhorned oxen disappear.

VIII. It is necessary that the bull with incipient horns should procreate descendants similarly equipped. It is undoubtedly in accordance with natural facts that he should do so. Still this philosophy is bound to tell us how came this law into existence, for it has the appearance of being a result of that intelligence, the existence of which it denies.

IX. Our incipient horn has yet to grow into a longer one, and then into a longer one, until it attains its full length. For this purpose, these processes of fightings and buttings, and throwing out of small variations and survivals of the strongest, besides ever-recurring favourable contingencies, have to be repeated times without number. To evade these difficulties, our only resource is again and again to brandish our magic talisman of infinite time.

X. As yet this long and painful process has only led to the evolution of horned individuals, and not a horned race. We must therefore invoke the theory of sexual selection, and suppose that the horned females fall in love with the horned appendage of their male companions. It is not easy for us to say what are the precise ideas which cows entertain of beauty. We know, however, that it is far from an invariable fact that the most handsome men and women unite in matrimony. Still, however, the assumption must be made, that the horned bull is irresistibly attractive to the horned cow before a horned species can be finally established by the forces at the service of this philosophy.

82. It is hardly possible to go through these successions of indefinite eons of time, and of concurrences of lucky chances with gravity, and suppose that they constitute a true account of the past history of the race of long-horned oxen. But the consequence which I deduce from it is a perfectly grave one. Few operations of nature can have been more simple than the evolution of a horn. But if by the aid of these forces alone the operation must have been so complicated, involving indefinite eons of time, and the casual concurrence of multitudes of happy chances, for its accomplishment, what must we say of the period requisite for the production of the other peculiarities of the race of oxen? What must we say of the infinitude of them, which must have been necessary for the production of all the complicated organisms and adaptations of animal life? This philosophy affirms that the bodily, intellectual, and moral nature of the most highly gifted man has been slowly evolved by a few unintelligent forces in a long line of ancestry from a simple cell. Will it endeavour to compute the number of distinct species which must have been evolved in this long succession; the number of eons which must have elapsed before each stage could have been accomplished? or the number of happy chances which must have concurred before each step could have become a possibility? When it has done this, let it multiply these arrays of figures, which it is scarcely possible to embody in any finite conception, and present us with the result? Surely this philosophy has stumbled on the regions of miracle without observing it. Far more miraculous is this mode of evolving the universe than the intervention of an intelligent Creator.

83. The number of intersections of independent forces, directed by nothing but blind laws, which this system is compelled to postulate, is alone sufficient to destroy its claim to be received as a philosophy. We know, as a matter of fact, that the occurrence of one lucky chance is a reason for expecting that it will not occur again; but this system is compelled to postulate them in endless succession. What right has it to make unlimited drafts on the infinite past, or the infinite future? What can positive science have to say to either of them? To affirm that blind forces can effect all things, if they have only sufficient time in which to operate, is not to propound a philosophy, but its negation. Our author, however, is not insensible to the difficulties with which he has to struggle. "It was doubtless," he says, "no small achievement, when, in yon ape-like horde, which we must consider as the cradle of the human race, the thoroughly erect posture became the fashion, instead of the waddle or partially developed gait of the higher apes; but step by step it went on improving, and time at least was no consideration. . . . . More astonishing still does this progress appear, from the harsh scream of the ape to articulate human speech."

84. Yes, doubtless, vast is the gulf which separates the two, for it involves the entire interval which separates the rational from the irrational, the self-conscious from the non-self-conscious, the capacity of moral obligation from the absence of it. Strauss is well aware that without language as an instrument, all real thought is impossible. He therefore summons to his aid a race or races of intermediate beings, of whose existence the evidence is *nil*, and supposes that they have existed. He also observes that monkeys have a kind of language, although he candidly admits that, whatever else they are capable of being taught (and they can be taught many things), they have never learned to speak, even when they have been brought into the closest contact with man. Nor has our constant companion, the dog, with his half-rationality and his apparent desire to give utterance to his feelings, made the smallest approach to the use of articulate speech, although he has been the friend of man for thousands of years. If a pantheistic or an atheistic philosopher could educate either the dog or monkey to use rationally even the lowest elements of human language, he would do more to prove his theory than by millions of conjectures.

85. But, adds our author, "Ere that prehuman branch little by little elaborated something of a language, periods of immeasurable duration may have elapsed; but after he had once hit upon speech, in however imperfect a condition, the speed of his progress was vastly accelerated," &c.

86. I ask emphatically, is it reasoning, to have recourse to the magic talisman of infinite time, as the solution of every difficulty? Is it not more rational to invoke the aid of an intelligent Creator? If it be replied that an intelligent Creator belongs to the regions of the unknowable, does not an inexhaustible past eternity equally belong to them? Does it not leave the origin of intelligence utterly unsolved?

87. Our author justly remarks, that if the power of thought fills us with astonishment, that of feeling is no less marvellous. "A divine force," says he, "reveals itself in the sensations of the lowest animal as much as in the brain of a Newton." After giving utterance to this great truth, a number of reasonings follow, for the purpose of proving that neither the one nor the other is divine. "If," says he, "under certain conditions, motion can be transformed into heat, why may it not, under other conditions, be transformed into thought, into sensation, or even into self-conscious reason and will?" Why, indeed? Because the one class of phenomena are entirely different from the other. Any philosophy worthy of the name ought to give proof of its assumed facts, instead of taking them for granted, by asking others to prove their impossibility.

88. This school of philosophy is forced to admit that there are certain organisms which are formidable obstacles in the way of elaborating the universe without the aid of an intelligent Creator. Of these, the eye may be taken as a crucial instance. "It is formed," says Strauss, "not in the light, but in the darkness of the womb, yet it is admirably adapted to light which has had no concern in its formation." A similar difficulty is well put by another writer, quoted by our author, respecting the instincts of animals. "These latter enable them to perform from their birth, with hereditary finished art, to which the highest reason might have prompted them for their well-being, without any thought, experience, or practice on their part, or any instruction, example, or pattern." Pantheism endeavours to account for this by assuming the presence of unconscious intellect in the universe.

89. Let it be observed that our sole experience of intellect is as an attribute of conscious beings. If philosophy is to rest on a basis of fact, the existence of unconscious intellect diffused in the universe is a gratuitous assumption. No doubt many intellectual processes take place in our minds without leaving any trace on the memory; perhaps without emerging into direct consciousness. This is especially the case with such actions as have become habitual. But this affords no proof of the presence of intellect in a wholly different class of beings. If unconscious

intellect can exist independently of any thinking subject, and aid in the construction of organisms, it follows that it must be inherent in every particle of matter of which they are composed. Also, that these unconscious intellectual atoms must have the faculty of acting in unison for the production of a common end ; and from the various means by which it may be accomplished, of selecting the most suitable. The bare statement of such a proposition is its most effectual refutation.

90. Next, our author invokes a theory of an unconscious absolute, which, "acting in all atoms, and organisms, as a universal soul, determines the contents of creation, and the evolution of the universe, by a ' Clairvoyant Wisdom,' superior to all consciousness." Such a theory may safely be consigned to the regions of dreary mysticism, though it is one which was hardly to be expected from one who imagines that he has escaped from the regions of the miraculous, by eliminating the conception of God from his philosophy.

91. But to enable him to account for the production of beings endowed with these faculties our author supplements these two principles by a theory of inherited habits, transmitted through a long line of ancestors, which have been gradually accumulated through indefinite successions of eons. "It is not," says he, "the seeing individual which forms its own, or its offspring's, eyes by acting in concert with light . . . . . the individual finds itself put into possession of an instrument which its predecessors, during immemorial time, have gradually brought to an ever higher grade of perfection." Again, "It is not our present bee which plans its skilful constructions, neither is it instructed in them by a Deity ; but in the lapse of thousands of years, since the lowest instincts were gradually developed into the various forms of Hymenoptera, the increasing needs produced by the struggle for existence have gradually fashioned these acts, which are now transmitted without effort as heirlooms to the present generation."

92. In the case of the eye there are two problems which require a definite solution, and we must not have our mental vision distracted from the point at issue by any phantasmagoria of words. First, the admirable adjustments and adaptations of the instrument itself—How come they? Secondly, How has this instrument, formed in total darkness, become perfectly correlated to the properties of light? There is one solution of these problems quite simple, and fully adequate to account for the facts—the existence of a God of boundless power and match-less skill, and fully acquainted with all resources and the end to be attained, who has framed the mechanism and adjusted it to external nature.

93. But there is also the solution of Pantheism and Atheism. Some of the simplest forms of life in the shape of cells burst into existence we know not how. These in the course of indefinite eons developed themselves into organisms of the simplest character, and these into others of endless variety impelled by blind forces alone; these grew into more perfect forms in the struggle for existence. Though why, until life had become abundant, there should have been any struggle at all it is hard to conceive. A power of sensation originated somehow, but how or whence we have no means of telling. These beings gradually differentiated themselves;—but how, whence, or where this power originated, or how each became possessed of another power, that of propagating its like—this philosophy is silent. After long courses of indefinite eons, a general power of sensation, diffused throughout the entire animal, concentrated itself in special senses, and produced the lowest form of eyes. Eon after eon rolled on its relentless course; variation arose after variation. Struggles for existence were ever ready to destroy imperfect specimens; at length one of the most perfect forms of eyes emerges. But all this leaves the problems with which we started utterly unaccounted for, viz., whence has originated the adaptations of the instrument itself; and how, being formed in darkness, has it become perfectly adapted to external light.

94. With respect to the origin of instincts, our philosophers take refuge in a theory of transmitted habits during something like an eternity of time. Step by step they have grown from the smallest origin, and by gradual accretions have been handed down from remote ancestors until they have assumed their present form. But if this were conceivable, the question arises, How came habits to be thus transmissible? Is it the result of the action of blind forces or of intelligence? Again, why is it that the inherited habits of instinctive intelligence, which must have been possessed by multitudes of ancestors in the long line of man's pedigree, have not been transmitted to him; but in this respect he is utterly distanced by the inferior animals? Let it be observed, that it is not a single instinct which has to be accounted for, but numbers numberless, spread over the wide regions of animated nature, and each adapted to the external circumstances of the animal.

95. The philosophy which we are considering is never wearied with urging the objection that our conception of a personal God is nothing more nor less than a magnified man. A very popular writer has recently had the bad taste to assert that the belief in a personal God differs little from a magnified Lord Shaftesbury. Such a question is one far too grave to be settled by ridicule.

96. It is perfectly true, that as long as man is man he can only represent truth in human conceptions. No less so is it that multitudes of his conceptions are inadequate representations of the realities beyond. If our reasonings were to be confined to conceptions which are adequate representations of things, they would be few indeed. The truth is, there is a law of our intellectual being which compels us to transcend the limits of the finite, and to assert that there must exist something beyond our highest conceptions of it. It is the very condition of thought.

97. But this philosophy affirms that the conception of a being who is at the same time personal and infinite involves a direct contradiction, and that a philosophy which asserts the existence of a personal God must be rotten at its foundations.

98. It is perfectly true that we have no experience of personality except as an attribute of finite beings. Let us inquire what we mean when we affirm that we are persons. A being who is a person is one who can predicate "I" of himself, who is conscious that he is distinct from all other persons, and non-persons, whose identity is preserved throughout all changes, and through protracted intervals of time, who feels himself to be a free agent, and is the subject of moral affections. There is no reason why an infinite being should not be capable of all these. The objection would be equally valid against introducing infinite quantities into calculations, because all our conceptions are finite. These, however, exist for the practical operations of mathematicians.

99. There is no doubt that the habit of theologians of reasoning about the infinite in the abstract, and not in the concrete, has involved the whole controversy in serious difficulties. What do we really mean when we assert that God is infinite? I answer that He is a being who transcends our highest thoughts, and that He is something beyond which we cannot fathom; that there is no point of space where His energy is not present; that there is nothing which is possible, which He cannot effect; nor any knowledge which He does not possess. His moral attributes ought to be designated perfect rather than infinite. The conception of infinite is quantitive, a moral one has nothing to do with quantity. Perfection, not infinitude, is properly applied to our ideas of justice, holiness, truthfulness, benevolence. The conception of a personal being, who in this sense is both infinite and perfect, plainly involves no contradiction; and is evidently not unthinkable, though our conception of Him may be inadequate.

100. Now, while it is a law of our nature that all our ideas must be human ones, there is no possible reason why they may

not represent attributes of other beings as well as of ourselves. If I see an animal perform actions of a certain character, I am justified in drawing the conclusion that they are the results of intelligence, although I am only acquainted by actual experience with human intelligence. I infer justly that the animal mind possesses in these respects an intelligence similar to my own. If, then, I can conceive of an imperfect form of intelligence, and reason on the fact, why may I not attribute our highest powers, freed from the imperfections with which they exist in man, to God? To assert that such an act is merely to manufacture a gigantic Lord Shaftesbury is not to appeal to reason, but to the worst feelings of our nature.

101. Nothing more clearly shows the impotency of this philosophy to grapple with the difficulties in which it is involved than the necessity it is under to use language which contradicts the truth of its own assumptions. Our author endeavours to apologise for the practice: "In so far as we speak," says he, "of a purpose in the universe, we are clearly conscious that we are expressing ourselves subjectively, and that we only express by it what we seem to recognize as the general result of the co-operation of the entire powers of the world."

102. In one word, all such expressions are blinds to enable us to impose on ourselves. A purpose in the universe is no purpose. It exists only in a delusive fancy of our subjective selves. Numbers of similar conceptions made use of by this philosophy can only exist as attributes of personality, and are utterly inapplicable to an impersonal something, whether we designate it Universe or God.

103. Yet our author writes as follows:—"The general deduction from the existence of the universe appears to be, as a whole, the most varied motion or the greatest abundance of life; this motion or life specialized as one developing itself morally as well as physically, struggling outwards and upwards, and even in the decline of the individual only preparing a new uprising."

104. Such language is a plain stultification of the principles on which this philosophy is based. Still more remarkable is the following passage:—"From our standpoint the object of the terrene development seems much nearer its attainment now, when the earth is filled by men and their works .... than many thousands of years ago, and when she was still exclusively occupied by mollusca and cretacea, to which fish were added later, then the mighty saurians with their allied species, and, finally, the primeval mammals, yet without man."

105. What object? I ask; for an impersonal Cosmos can have none. Is man, then, the end of creation, its complement and crown? Is the purpose of an impersonal Cosmos getting near its realization? Unless this philosophy utters absolute nonsense, it has arrived at the same conclusion as Theism, that a purpose exists somewhere in the universe. Common sense must draw the conclusion that a purpose can exist only in a personal intelligence, i.e. in God.

106. But there is a future which this philosophy must face, and which the mind of man, despite of all philosophy, will inquire into with the profoundest interest. What, then, are the destinies of the Cosmos? What are the future prospects of man as an individual and a race? Let us hear the answer which it returns. "Nevertheless a time must come when the earth will be no longer inhabited; nay, when we shall have ceased to exist as a planet. Then all which in the course of her development was produced, and in a manner accomplished by her—all living and rational beings and all their productions, all political organizations, all works of art and science—will not only necessarily have vanished from existence without a trace, but even the memory of them will survive in no mind, as the history of the earth must necessarily perish with her."

107. Surely this is a dark prospect which this philosophy unfolds. Man, as an individual, and as a race, shall pass into eternal silence; and no trace of him or his works shall remain in any mind. Still, if this is the inevitable destiny of the future, let us face it boldly and honestly; and not imitate the ancient philosopher, who wished, if the doctrine of man's immortality were not true, that no one should undeceive him while he lived. No; if this philosophy is true, the most cultivated intellects, the greatest moral elevation, and the lowest baseness of wickedness, shall alike rest in peaceful, but eternal silence.

108. Again, "Either the earth," says the author, "has missed her aim here—no result has been produced by her protracted existence—or this aim did not consist in something which was intended to endure, but has been attained at every moment of her development." Let us take courage then, for the gospel of despair can only express itself in the terms of the gospel of hope. Nature, then, has an aim and a purpose! Aims and purposes are not attributes of an impersonal infinity, but of intelligence, personality, and will. It also announces that the infinite All perishes not, nor ceases from its perfection. "The All in no succeeding moment is more perfect than in the preceding one, nor vice versâ. There exists in it, in fact, no

such distinction as sooner or later, because all gradations and successions, stages of contraction and expansion, ascent and decline, becoming and perishing, exist side by side, mutually supplementing one another to infinity." This, then, is our consolation. Though we perish, the mighty All remains unchanged in its perfection. The elements of which we are composed may, during the evolutions of eternity, help to build up glorious galaxies, though of ourselves, as conscious individuals, there shall be no resurrection.

109. There is something in human nature too strong for the reasonings of pantheistic and atheistic philosophy to crush. Danton, when questioned at his last trial as to his abode, replied, " My abode shall soon be annihilation ; but I shall live in the pantheon of history." This philosophy teaches that even this hope is only a fond delusion. What are the substitutes it furnishes to satisfy the eager cravings of the human heart ? Ah ! a reverent regard for a Cosmos for which it is impossible to feel either reverence or regard. The memory of a departed wife, to be to us in place of a religion ; the worship of humanity, typified in a female form, the destruction of which humanity is certain. This is its substitute for a personal God, the moral governor of the universe, which He has created ; whose attributes are justice, mercy, and truth ; whose providence embraces all His works ; who shall continue reigning for ever and ever. Religion teaches an hereafter, which shall give a scope for the exercise of man's mighty powers, which is denied him here. But this philosophy affirms that one destiny awaits the holiest and the most abandoned, the man of the most disinterested benevolence and the most refined cruelty, a Nero and a St. Paul—a silence from which there shall be no awakening—the conscious being of both alike shall be swallowed up in the infinite Cosmos. The only conclusion of such a philosophy must be, let each man enjoy life as he best can, for we shall die to-morrow, and sleep for ever the sleep of unconsciousness. The best safeguard against such a philosophy is, that human nature will refuse to accept it as a true account of its aims, its aspirations, and its destinies.

The CHAIRMAN. I am sure that I shall fulfil your desires by expressing our thanks to Mr. Row for his very ably reasoned out paper. Some letters will now be read by the Honorary Secretary.

The Hon. SECRETARY. The first letter which I have to read is from the Ven. Archdeacon W. LEE, D.D.. Professor of Divinity at Trinity College, Dublin.

11

" My dear Sir,   " April 12th, 1874.
      " Mr. Row's paper is excellent, and is remarkably successful in
embracing within a very limited space a very large field indeed of con-
troversial matter. It is calculated to be most useful, and I desire to bear
my humble tribute of assent to the soundness of the conclusions maintained,
and of the principles upon which they are grounded.
      " I thank you much for allowing me to study this valuable paper, and I
congratulate your Society on having the privilege of giving to the world
so powerful an antidote to the unbelieving tendences of Positivism and
Pantheism.
                                 " I remain, faithfully yours,
" Capt. F. W. H. Petrie."   " WILLIAM LEE.

Rev. Canon MOZLEY, D.D., Regius Professor of Divinity at Oxford,
writes as follows :—
                                                   " April 18th, 1874.
      " I have read with the greatest interest the Victoria Institute
paper, which is full of important thought upon the question of the day.
The discussion of the Darwin question seems to be especially able, and
charged with strong argument upon the turning-points. The resort of a
blind infinity, to which everything is referred, and which is thought to carry
off any amount of contrivance under the shape of chances (of which it in-
cludes an infinite number), is admirably exposed. The paper shows, with great
power, that contrivance cannot be identical with an infinite chaos of jostling
chances, one going against another ; and that an infinity of time does *not*
give you a reasonable foundation of apparent works of design,—if there is
nothing to be taken into account but that, to reduce a confusion and medley
of blind laws to order.
      " The terrible melancholy of Strauss's system must, one would think,
limit its adoption to the most determined of the despairing school. He
seems to grasp with considerable power in his mind, the frightful end of
annihilation, as he maintains it, and to make that power which he exerts
a consolation to him for the dreadful truth, as he regards it ; but it is a
barren consolation indeed.
                                 " I am, yours very truly,
                                                  " J. B. MOZLEY."

The Rev. Prebendary COLERIDGE writes : —
                                                   " April 11th, 1874.
      " I have read Mr. Row's able paper with much interest, and very
general approval. I shall not be able to be present at the discussion, and
even if I had more time at my disposal, I feel that any remarks of mine
would scarce be worth the attention of the meeting.
      " As regards the great question at issue, my main reliance under God is :—
" First, on the *zeal*, the *discretion*, and the religious *wisdom* of the
Christian ministry ; on their good example and personal influence.
Christianity, truly and rationally exhibited, shines by its own light ; while
as regards pure theism, the Gospel of Christ, in its fulness and purity, I
believe to be at once the best exponent, and the only safe guardian, of the
great fundamental truth which it pre-supposes and embodies.
      " Secondly, in the spread of a spiritual philosophy, not set forth in overt
opposition to the materialistic tendencies of the age, - rather embracing and
welcoming the discoveries of modern science, though placing them in a truer
and fuller light,—a philosophy underlying what now assumes, too exclusively,
the name of science—*scientia scientiarum*.
      " Still, there may be need of direct controversy in the way, whether of

attack or defence ; and here there needs, what is too often wanting, a thorough understanding of the adversary's stand-point, his arguments, and conclusions, with a manifest disposition to do justice both to him and to his views : not to aim at a mere argumentative triumph ; not to take advantage of any accidental slip or error in his ratiocination ; rather to place the position combated in the best light of which it is susceptible : not to trust too much to the argument *ex concesso* or *ad hominem*. The cause may be right, though the pleading be weak ; and, in fact, the good cause has suffered far more from its friends than from its assailants. In a word, to seek *truth*, and we are told to seek peace, as to ensue it, impartially, if not dispassionately.

"And, when all is done, any belief in God worth contending for, must, in my judgment, rest upon a ground of *faith*. There must be a suitable attitude and energy of the *will*,—a *moral* element, which cannot and ought not to be eliminated.

" It may be added, that the most telling arguments against the truth of religion, whether natural or revealed,—that is to say, Scriptural,—lie out of the domain of physics. They are either metaphysical, or, much more commonly, of a moral nature, and appeal to the conscience. It is with these that we have mainly to deal.

"Mr. Row's assault upon the Darwinian hypothesis is very powerful ; and it is remarkable that one strong objection,—want of time,—has been anticipated, but not answered, by Darwin himself. But the question is not vital, however Strauss may have regarded it. Whatever the *process* may be, the result is not less admirable, nor the original less divine. Such inquiries into the course of nature may be examined with entire equanimity. The mystery of creation is not hereby solved, nor the divine truth any way compromised.

"As regards *causation*, my impression is that John S. Mill was latterly opposed to Comte on this point, and that he recognized a true causality. Anyhow, I entirely agree with the lecturer.

"I am, &c.,

" DERWENT COLERIDGE, M.A., Prebendary of St. Paul's."

The Rev. Prebendary GRIFFITHS says :—

"April 10th, 1874.

" SIR,—I regret that I am unable to be present at the reading of Mr. Row's paper, but avail myself of your invitation to give utterance to some thoughts of which it is suggestive.

" I.—And first. The quotations from Strauss appear to me striking instances of what I conceive to be the fundamental fallacy which pervades the whole school of thought of which he constitutes himself the mouthpiece ; namely, the deluded and delusive worship of mere empty words. With them, as Caro says, ' les mots prennent la place des êtres ; l'axiome *Nomina Numina* est à la lettre une vérité pour ces nouvelles écoles.' Thus we find them substituting adjectives for substantives ; relations of things for things related ; appearances for things apparent.

" 1. Take their first principle (paper, sec. 9), that ' all our knowledge is merely phenomenal.' This very fact, instead of justifying our stopping short at the phenomenal, suggests, and by the laws of our mind obliges, the recognition of *things*—realities—underlying this phenomenal. For ' phenomenal ' is an adjective, and ' phenomena ' equally an adjectival term, has no meaning till you supply the suppressed substantives. And these substantives force themselves on our notice from two different sides ; you must complete the phrase by the admission of an *object* or objects or which phenomena are phenomenal, and of a *subject* or subjects TO which they are phenomenal. The images in a mirror are phenomenal; but they, by the very force of the word, imply objects *of which* they are the reflection, and a subject *to whom* they reflect their objects. To speak of 'phenomena' taken alone is as absurd as it would be to speak of 'greennesses' instead of things green. And universally, a 'phenomenal' world does not exclude, but by the very adjectival nature of the term implies and demands, the recognition of non-phenomenal realities which present these phenomena to a reality which perceives them. 'No appearance without reality,' is a principle which Herbart has thoroughly established in his *Hauptpunkte der Metaph.* and throughout his works.

"2. A similar sophism runs through Strauss's words in (paper, sec. 43). 'We must regard the creation as the laboratory of the reasonable and the good.' The phrase is perfectly empty, unless you fill it up with its proper contents, 'reasonable and good *things*.' And reasonable and good *things* can have their origin only in a reasonable and good *person* of whom they are the emanation, and who has (to use Strauss's own words) 'a disposition to the reasonable and the good.'

"3. Again, when it is affirmed (paper, sec. 56) that life is 'nothing but a form of motion,' the question immediately presents itself, 'but what is motion?' Motion is not a *thing per se*, but simply a term expressing a *relation* of things—a state of *relation* between things. It implies therefore and demands the recognition of *things* (entities) existing in certain relations to each other, the *changes* in which relations are manifested to us in the *form* of motion. There must be life, or lives, existent, in order to present to our eyes this '*form*' or these varying '*forms*' of existence which we designate as 'motion.'

"In short, on this whole subject M. Caro's answer to M. Taine is irresistible : 'Qu'on essaye de concevoir ce que serait un *fait* s'il n'y avait pas *d'êtres*, un *phénomène* s'il n'y avait pas *d'existences*. 'Nous ne saisissons,' dit M. Taine, 'que des *couleurs*, des *sons*, des *résistances*, des *mouvements*.' Mais la couleur, le son, la résistance, le mouvement, voilà certes les plus inintelligibles des abstractions si vous n'entendez pas *quelque chose* qui est coloré, sonore, mû et résistant, ou bien encore si vous ne concevez pas ce rapport particulier entre telle *chose extérieure* et le *moi* qui constitue la sensation de couleur, de son, de mouvement, et de résistance.' (Caro, *l'Idée de Dieu*, p. 165.)

"II.—In regard to the theory of Evolution, I hold that it has as much consistency with Theism as any notions of 'creation' hitherto held. For 'Evolution' seems to me only a wider generalization, from wider premisses, of the notion of *production*. And it matters not through how many or how few stages this production runs. Our views of the *mode* of production must vary with our insight into the processes of nature ; but the *fact* of production remains the same. All processes, mediate or immediate, are still the processes of an ever-present and originative Deity. God always *is*. 'My father works without intermission up to this present moment, and I similarly so work.' The *vis genetrix* (the Father) and the *vis formativa* (the Son) are constants (John v. 17).

"III.—Once more I would suggest, in connection with sections 98, 99, that it seems to me a hasty assumption of our opponents, too generally conceded, that '*Personality*' involves of necessity the antithesis between self and not-self ; the predication of 'I' in conscious distinction from 'not I' (sec. 98). Animals have clearly this distinction ; they are individuals, and feel themselves to be individuals as much as we do ; yet animals have not what we mean by Personality. The essence of Personality I am disposed to place (with I. H. Fichte, who has elaborated the point) in the power of self-inspection and self-regulation ; the ability to take in by the mental glance the whole compass of our conceptions, in their proper order and associations, and to govern ourselves at all times, in all things, in accordance with this comprehensive view. In this sense, individuals attain Personality only in proportion to such self-knowledge and self-government, and the divine Being, so far from being incapable of such Personality, is the only Entity in whom it perfectly exists.

"I therefore fully agree with Mr. Row (see. 99) in deprecating the use of the abstractions—'infinite,' 'absolute,' &c., as applied to this divine Being. It is only by analogy that we can speak or think of Him at all ; and this analogy we can borrow from no other quarter but our own nature, seeing that this nature is incontestably the highest known to us. In cases where men were more degenerate, they often represented their Deities under terms borrowed from animal superiority ; but in proportion as we are human, we can fitly conceive God only in terms of the human : as the Image of God in us makes itself clear we can (reciprocally) *think* God only after the image of man. We must conceive Him as the perfect Model of those highest qualities which glimmer in us imperfectly ; and this, too, in the *order* in which these qualities unfold themselves. Whence, in successive stages of human development the Deity is figured, mainly, at one time as the All-Powerful ; at another as the All-Wise ; at another (as the culminating point of the idea) as the All-Good.

"I am, &c.
"THOMAS GRIFFITH, Prebendary of St. Paul's."

The CHAIRMAN.—It is an exceedingly happy circumstance that Mr. Row has brought before us so clearly the tendency of the philosophy of Mill, and also that of Strauss. Perhaps Mr. Row has been less successful in grappling with Dr. Darwin's views, and in stating the views of the objectors to his theory ; for I do not suppose any one who is acquainted with Dr. Darwin would accuse him of *intentional* atheism or of pantheism. What the result of his theory may be is another matter, concerning which I have a strong judgment of my own. But I conceive from all I have noticed in studying Dr. Darwin, that he has formed his theory independently of the question as to whether there was any Supreme God or not,—not taking the trouble, if I may so speak, to decide logically that question. He always speaks with a kind of reverence of the Almighty ; and in his theory the Almighty holds a place which has been objected to by some as being extremely illogical ; for he brings in the notion of the Almighty, but it is such an Almighty that when we come to consider the idea we find it is not the Omnipotent Being of either Christianity, Judaism, or Mahometanism. It is a being who, having given rise to, and originated certain creations, seems to have lapsed into silence, very much like the Indian Brahm, who finished up by producing an egg which shone like ten thousand worlds ; out of which egg was produced Brahma, the active intelligence : and that active intelligence had to have his works perfected by the Indian Vulcan, who wrought everything into perfect order. The notion that Darwin brings before us, of natural selection, certainly involves a personality always and continually at work. That personality many persons suppose to be a divine power ; but then it is a strange conception of a divine power that that power should be attendant upon a series of changes and chances ; and that when a good change is made which produces an improvement, divine power should be always ready to pick up the change which opportunity thus offers, and to perpetuate it for the future. All this theory seems to me so very illogical that I cannot conceive how it is that persons of intelligence can be satisfied with it. But it is not atheism, nor is it pantheism, although to my mind it is something more like polytheism than either.

Mr. CADMAN JONES.—There is only one point to which I should like to call attention, and that is a mathematical one with which I happen to be familiar. There has been brought forward here what all mathematicians would pronounce to be a mathematical heresy. It occurs twice,—first in the 37th paragraph, where it is stated that, "as far as experience goes, lucky chances have no tendency to repeat themselves. On the contrary, the legitimate inference is that the occurrence of one once, is a reason why we should expect it not to occur again." Then it is repeated in the 83rd paragraph, "We know, as a matter of fact, that the occurrence of one lucky chance is a reason for expecting it not to occur again." Now, according to the theory of chances, let us take the instance of twelve dice, and suppose that they were perfectly fair, so that on an average each die would bring up its ace once in six throws. If they fell all aces at the first throw there would be no reason, from its happening that time, why it should not be just as likely to happen again upon the next throw. It is a most improbable event that they should turn up all aces, but, assuming the dice fair, whatever the probability was at the first throw there is just the same probability at the second. The only way in which the fact that they all came up aces the first time bears upon the probability that they will all come up aces on the second throw, is that it raises an inference that they were loaded. On this ground if a certain contingency happens once, it is rather more likely then that it will happen a second time than it was before the first occasion. If it happens several times successively, the probability is considerably increased. I notice this point, because I think Mr. Row is pushing the argument a little further than he ought when he states that the occurrence of a lucky chance is a reason for expecting it not to repeat itself.

The Rev. Prebendary IRONS, D.D.—Would not that entirely change the conditions of the probability ? When Mr. Jones assumes that directly the dice have fallen in the manner suggested, he should come to the conclusion that they were plugged, or not fair dice, he changes his hypothesis at once. I require him to keep his hypothesis as it was, that the dice should be fair dice, and that they should fall in the way suggested, and then I think the doctrine of chances would be rather against him.—I must express my sense of obligation to Mr. Row, whose paper is full of thought, though it does not pretend to exhaust the whole subject. We are bound to recognize thankfully that it will enable all persons who care to do so, to reason out many parts of Strauss's metaphysics, in a way that no other paper which I have seen has yet done. With reference to the general subject, I think the fact is a startling and painful one, that such a philosophical theory as that of Strauss (and not Strauss's only) should be so popular in these days ; and we ought to ask ourselves how it happens that Christianity, having had possession in the world, having had the field greatly in its own hands for so long a time, should have admitted such an intellectual development as that which we notice in the present day. Surely there must be some grave blot among us, that such a thing could be possible. Is it not that we have been content to soften down the distinctive philosophy of our religion, and accept a very vague and thin theism, instead of the doctrines of Christian theology ; and that that has led men to stray into those indistinct shallows, where the faith of many young and untaught persons will unfortunately be lost ? The fault is clearly our own ; and it can only be removed by our endeavouring, hereafter, not to be so much afraid of deep inquiries* as some people are. Even the conception of a personal God—the idea of Him in whom we live, and move, and have our being —has been so vaguely contemplated among us for several generations, and especially in our own time, that I can scarcely wonder that things have come to this pass. For the whole of the work of the Christian Church for the first 500 years was intended to clear in the mind of Christians the truth of the Trinity and, in some degree, even the ontology of that awful Being with whom we have to do. The true doctrine of the Godhead, as the very fountain and object of our worship, was proclaimed, as far as human language and thought will admit definition. But after Athanasius lived, and his great work was done, there was an intellectual pause ; and as we, in our days, have fallen back on anthropology, and have rather dimmed our theology, we must take the consequences. Some of these consequences are to be seen in the writings of Strauss and his followers. If we look back, and contemplate the time when this creation was not, we come at once to the greatest difficulty of all theology, the fact that He, who had not created us, began to create. We have to conceive, as St. Athanasius pointed out, how it was possible for the infinite God to begin that form of action for the first time, which we call creation, without any change in Himself ; for we hold Him to be unchangeable. We cannot struggle through this problem without a thoughtful ontology ; and that at the present day is despised as too dogmatic. But people must come back to dogma, and to the conclusions of the Christian schools,—if they do not wish to end with such men as Strauss and Mill.

The Rev. Dr. CURREY.—I do not feel equal to entering upon a discussion of a paper that contains so much matter for thought as this one, for which we are deeply indebted to Mr. Row. I merely rise to call attention to an occurrence which took place in Germany some thirty-three years ago, which shows how the natural instincts of men speak in favour of the existence of a God. The account is to be found in Hundeshagen's *Deutsche Protestantismus*, who quotes from a report, given by an unbeliever, of a meeting which was held by

---

* Lord Bacon has remarked that "a smattering of philosophy leads to atheism ; whereas a thorough acquaintance with it, brings him back again to religion."—ED.

some of " the freest spirits " in Germany. Certain of those men met together for the purpose of discussing and proclaiming the choicest theories of the freest school of thought, and the witness recording the circumstance says, that one person rose, and after declaring several new views and theories, proclaimed distinctly his disbelief in the existence of a God. The writer goes on to say :—" I found at that time that his remark was ill placed, for though I entirely agree with what he said, still our education as yet is so imperfect, that we are not prepared to receive this statement in the naked form. The result was what I expected. A shudder, followed by a complete silence, passed over the whole assembly ; and this occurred in an assembly of the freest spirits of Germany. At last the thought, which I felt sure was in the minds of a large number of those present found vent in the speech of an honest Swabian, who rose up and with a trembling, but distinct voice said,—'Gentlemen, I cannot help expressing a thought that comes into my mind, whatever may be said of it. I have the greatest desire for freedom of thought, but still I cannot help declaring my firm belief that there is a God.' At these words a thrill passed through the whole assembly, a clattering of glasses followed, a shouting and uprising, and the whole assembly seemed as if they had found a friend whom they had lost." I think that this is a strong testimony, especially when we find it given by an unbeliever. (Cheers.)

The Rev. C. M. DAVIES, D.D. — I should like to have some one like Mr. Row with me on the platforms, where I find the atheists and secularists carrying everything before them ; for now the weakest possible theists and critics seem to be put forward as so many ninepins for Mr. Bradlaugh and his colleagues to knock down.

Mr. Row.—In replying to the discussion which has taken place, I may say that a very few observations are necessary, for the criticism upon my paper seems to have been confined to one point only. As to the subject of the dice, I treated that as a matter of common sense ; and I am sure of this, that if I were to produce a dozen dice, and every time I threw them they turned up aces, there could be but one opinion upon the subject. As an example, I know an instance in which a person had two Turkish bonds—one for £500, the other for £100—who actually, at one drawing, drew both. A broker told me that it was the most remarkable circumstance that had ever come under his notice. But if the owner of the bonds had gone on buying and drawing in the same way, you would have said that there was some cheating at work. Viewing the question as a practical fact, I am perfectly sure there is not a person who does not apprehend the nature of the argument which I used to exhibit the impossibility of these unusual concurrences in nature, which must take place if these theories are correct. A number of such concurrences is like the chances I have referred to, and they must intersect one another in certain points in numbers numberless to render these things possible. I have put it fairly in the point about the oxen ; here it is an actual necessity, that events should intersect at the right time and place ; and, supposing the herd had to encounter, not a set of animals capable of butting powerfully, but a set of horses, there would have been no tendency for the growth of the horn. But here you have to assume the perfected recurrence of favourable conditions, and so on for ever. I quoted the dice simply as an illustration. We all feel it is an impossibility for twelve dice to fall with their aces uppermost, and for this to be repeated, say one hundred times. This is the only point which has been objected to in my paper. These adaptations of nature exist in number, numberless; and I am certain the only adequate solution of them is, that the universe is loaded by Deity to bring about a corresponding result. My object has been to test the thing simply from the closest logical point of view, and to see whether these arguments of Strauss and others will bear argument. I think that my paper shows that they will not. Whatever may be said about the theory of evolution, I have distinctly laid it down that there are certain gaps in that theory which it is hopeless to attempt to bridge over. There is a self-consciousness, there is that in the moral nature of man which says "I ought." I do not wish to enter into a discussion about mutation; that was beside the object of my paper; but my object was to take certain data as laid down, and to ask, "Will the conclusions deduced from them legitimately follow?" I quite agree with Dr. Davies, who says that unbelievers are frequently confronted by men of straw, who do not know what they are talking about.

The Meeting was then adjourned.

REMARKS ON THE SUBJECT OF THE REV. PREBENDARY C. A. ROW'S PAPER,

By the Rev. Professor Challis, M.A., F.R.S., F.R.A.S.

In bringing before the members of the Institute the following remarks relative to the subject of Mr. Row's paper, namely, "The Principles of Modern Pantheistic and Atheistic Philosophy as exemplified in the last Works of Strauss and others," it is not my intention to criticise the views expressed in that paper, the general tenor of which I entirely assent to. I agree also, in almost every instance, with the particular arguments which Mr. Row has adduced in support of his views ; as well the arguments that rest on independent grounds, as those which attack the reasoning of the opponents on their own principles. The only reservation I have to make is, that I think the treatment of the subject is not as complete as it might be, and requires to be *supplemented*. In order to encounter effectually the philosophy of such reasoners as Strauss, Mill, Darwin, &c., it seems to me necessary, not only to expose the consequences of their reasonings, but also to inquire how their modes of thought have *originated*. This inquiry, as I hope to show, turns upon the view that is taken of the essential character of *physical causation*. I ask, therefore, as having devoted a life both to the advancement of physical science by mathematics, and to the study of its fundamental principles, to be allowed to submit for consideration the following arguments :—

1. It is a singular circumstance, not generally recognized, that the philosophical systems of the above-mentioned writers have had their origin in the great step taken by Newton in physical science by the demonstration of the laws of gravitation. Newton proved that two bodies attract each other in proportion to their masses, and according to the law of the inverse square of the distance between them ; but did not *prove* that this attraction is effected by means of an *intervening* substance. He has, however, left on record that he fully believed in the existence of such intervention, and that he regarded as " incompetent in philosophy " any one who thought otherwise. Newton's discovery was the first instance of a step taken in a philosophy of *causes*, and gave rise to much speculation as to the quality of the force of gravity. Notwithstanding the expression by Newton of a contrary opinion, the occult quality of gravity came to be believed, and the *actio in distans*, as it is called by German physicists, was generally accepted. Thus it was admitted as a philosophical dogma, that a physical operation might be such as not only not to be understood from sensation and experience, but even to be *contradictory* to what we so understand ; for by sensation and experience we understand that body acts upon body by *contact and pressure*.

e

2. Taking advantage of the above-mentioned admission, Hume proposed in place of a theory of causation, the hypothesis of mere antecedence and consequence according to invariable law. This idea, which has been very generally adopted by modern metaphysicians, is virtually an abandonment of the reality of intelligible causation, and gives a kind of omnipotence to law. The denial of the possibility of miracles is a logical consequence of accepting it; and, in short, the same dogma forms the basis of all the sceptical and neological opinions that have in recent times prevailed so much in Germany and France, culminating, as it were, in the writings of Strauss and Renan.

3. The natural philosophy of which Newton laid the foundation, and indicated the rules (in Book III. of the "Principia"), leads, when legitimately applied, to conclusions in direct contradiction to Hume's principle of antecedence and consequence without assignable cause. Newton conceived that all the physical forces, inclusive of gravity, might be modes of action of a universal elastic medium (the *æther*), the sensible existence of which is now generally recognized. Such a medium acts necessarily by *pressure*, and, therefore, in a manner comprehensible by us, because we know by personal sensation and experience what pressure is. In fact, on the hypothesis that the æther is so constituted that variations of its pressure are always and everywhere proportional to variations of its density, all the modes of its action are such as come within the province of calculation by mathematics. It is thus known, for instance, how *light*, which is one form of physical force, travels by means of the æther uniformly with an immense velocity through illimitable space.

4. Besides the existence of the æther, the antecedents of physical science point to the fact that all visible and tangible substances are composed of indivisible parts, called *atoms*, to which, on the above view of the nature of the physical forces, there is no need to attribute any qualities other than inertia, and constancy of form and magnitude. The æther, the atoms, and the juxtaposition of atoms in definite arrangements and proportions so as to constitute the simpler natural bodies, being given, together with the intrinsic qualities of the æther and the atoms, all the elements for constructing the material universe are furnished, as well as all the data required for submitting to calculation the various operations by which it has been brought into its present condition, and is maintained therein. In short, according to this philosophy, all quantitative relations admit of being ascertained by mathematical reasoning; and the mere fact that the word "square" occurs in the enunciation of the law of gravity is evidence that the proof of the law is within the province of mathematical investigation. I am far from asserting that physical science has reached, or even approached, the completeness and comprehensiveness of which I have here supposed it to be capable; it is sufficient for my present purpose to have ground for saying that arguments drawn from its actual condition afford a reasonable presumption that the above statement correctly describes its essential character. (Such arguments will be found in my work on the "Principles

of Mathematics and Physics," which was published in 1869 ; and in a smaller work, entitled "An Essay on the Mathematical Principles of Physics," published in 1873.)

5. I am now prepared to indicate in what respect the Newtonian philosophy, legitimately employed, contradicts the assumption that phenomena can only be accounted for on the principle of mere antecedence and consequence according to law, and that, consequently, it is not possible to understand causes. From what is argued above, it will be seen that in direct contravention of that assumption, Newton's philosophy admits of the existence of no *consequence* the relation of which to an antecedent cause is not cognisable from common sensation and experience. If we had no other sense than that of sight, we might conclude that matter is capable of moving matter without the agency of an intervening substance. But the sense of touch, and our consciousness of will and power, enable us to perceive that matter is acted upon by the *pressure* of other matter in contact with it, and according to the principles of a philosophy which refers all knowledge to personal sensation and experience, no other mode of action is admissible.

6. It is true, however, that thus we do not account for the existence of the æther, the atoms, and the simpler substances composed of atoms, nor for their respective inherent qualities ; because, in fact, these entities constitute the *foundation* of the philosophy. The property of pressing proportionally to its density, which was considered (in Article 3) to belong to the æther, is quite intelligible from what we know of the sensible properties of visible and tangible fluids, in certain of which (as air of given temperature) the law actually exists. Now, although in the case of such bodies this law of pressure might be shown to be due to dynamical action of the æther, inasmuch as all the physical forces (as already argued in Article 4) are to be regarded as modes of its pressure, there is no need to seek for an analogous reason for the same law as respects the æther itself, because the hypothesis of this property is necessary as a foundation for applying mathematics to calculate its motions ; and the law, so far as it pertains to the æther, may be considered to be an ultimate fact.

7. Accordingly, there are *two kinds* of physical realities that human intelligence is capable of taking cognisance of,—those which as ultimate elements or facts constitute the basis of all physical phenomena, and those which are produced from these by causes operating according to ascertainable laws. It is evident that the first kind admit of inquiry only as to their qualities, not as regards any antecedent producing cause ; whereas the other kind are proper subjects of human investigation, both as to the causes producing them, and as to the laws or modes of operation of the causes. The one kind, as having no antecedents, only give evidence of creative power ; the other as consisting of antecedents and consequents, the relations between which are such as we can understand, furnish proofs to us of intelligence and wisdom. The intelligence is of the same kind, however different in degree, as that which the working of a machine which accomplishes in an intelligible manner

the purpose for which it was constructed gives of the skill and ability of its fabricator ; for it must be supposed that in calling the elements and their qualities into existence for effecting His purposes, the Creator had prevision of all those consequences from them which we seek to acquire a knowledge of by so much toil in experimental and mathematical research. From the foregoing considerations, it seems reasonable to conclude that the world was created so as to be in reality such as we perceive it to be for the purpose (among others) of making intelligible to us the wisdom, as well as the power, of the Creator ; and that for the same reason "all things have been ordered in number, measure, and weight." (For more that might be said on this part of the subject I beg to refer to the concluding portions of the two works I have already named.)

8. The possibility of a miracle, which the writers before mentioned refuse to admit, as being repugnant to the principles of their philosophy, is quite consistent with the views maintained above, according to which a miracle may be said to be performed by an exercise of power of the same kind as that which created the constituent elements of substances, and endued them with qualities, and which can, consequently, change them in any manner, and even destroy them. The extension of this power to the creating, altering, or destroying, the combinations and arrangements of atoms whereby organic as well as inorganic bodies are constituted, must be conceded to be possible on the principle that whilst from personal acts and consciousness we can understand what it is to make or create, we are wholly unable to assign limits to the creative power of the Maker of the universe. (I shall have occasion subsequently to cite this assertion.) Of course, a miracle, however performed, as being a superhuman act, is to be regarded as the act of the Creator and Upholder of all things, although human agency may have been concerned in the performance of it. It seems, in fact, to be sufficiently established by testimony that on particular occasions, and for special reasons, miracles have been wrought in answer to the prayers of righteous men gifted in a high degree with understanding and faith, but not the less are they wrought by the power of God.

9. The conclusion I draw from the preceding arguments is, that the πρῶτον ψεῦδος, or radical fault, in the commonly received systems of physics and metaphysics, lies in the acceptance of the doctrine of invariable antecedence and sequence, to the exclusion of the consideration of causes. This belief may be said (in words that occur in the Book of Wisdom) to be "a betrayal of the succours of reason." It seems, in fact, to influence in various and singular ways the intellectual faculty of those who hold it. Possibly we may thus account for the mental peculiarity which, as mentioned in Art. 8 of Mr. Row's paper, "considers it possible that in some distant region of the universe two and two may make five." Others of the same way of thinking have imagined it to be possible that somewhere space may have more dimensions than length, breadth, and depth. Another instance of false conception, having, it seems to me a like origin, is referred to in Art. 87 of Mr Row's essay as having been relied upon by Strauss for supporting some of

his metaphysical views, namely, the conception that, "under certain conditions motion can be transformed into heat." It is an undoubted axiom of natural philosophy that motion *per se* is just as incapable as *rest* is of producing motion. But heat is essentially a mode of force, and can produce motion. Hence heat and motion are heterogeneous entities, and inconvertible one into the other ; so that Strauss, misled apparently by reliance on faulty principles of philosophy, cited in support of his argument a physical impossibility.

10. But the most signal instance of irrational misconception is that of Hume himself, who failed to see that his system, by which he supposed miracle was excluded, requires a continual recurrence of miracles, inasmuch as a succession of events for which no intelligible cause is assignable is, for that reason alone, miraculous. There are, however, physical circumstances to which Hume's principle of mere antecedence and consequence strictly applies, which, in fact, I had occasion to discuss in the communication I had the honour of making to the Institute on the 5th of last January. I allude to the circumstances that sensations of musical sounds are immediately preceded by vibrations of the air, as are those of colour by vibrations of the æther, although the relation between the sensations and the operative physical conditions is one of mere antecedence and consequence, inasmuch as by no human cognisance or research could it be anticipated that such antecedents would have such consequents. The sensational consequents are such as they are by the immediate volition of the Author of our being, and, therefore, come under the category of miracle.

11. I propose now to say a few words on the principles of Darwinism. The chief remark I have to make on this subject is, that the same radical fault runs through Darwinism as that I have pointed out as being involved in the received physical theories,—the fault of not making the proper distinction between what has received existence by immediate creation, and what has been derived therefrom by causes operating according to intelligible laws. There is, however, this remarkable difference, that whereas in physics too little has been ascribed to evolution,—the derivation, for instance, of the law of gravity from antecedently-created conditions having been overlooked or denied,—in Darwinism, on the contrary, so much has been ascribed to natural development that the idea of antecedent creation is almost got rid of.

12. The following arguments apply directly to the organisms of plants, but *mutatis mutandis* may be taken to apply to those of animals. Naturalists tell us that the most elementary constituents of organic matter, whether the organism be in a state of growth or decay, are hollow vesicles, or *cells*. Let this be granted as admitting of experimental determination. But how a combination of cells, which have apparently no inherent principle of vitality, might *originate seed*, we are not told. Sir William Thomson, when President of the British Association at Edinburgh in 1871, broached the hypothesis that seeds might be conveyed to the earth by aërolites projected from distant planets, or other cosmical bodies ; whereupon every one, scientific and non-

scientific, exclaimed, " This shifts the difficulty without removing it, for the existence of these extra-mundane seeds is still to be accounted for." The circumstance that so eminent a scientific investigator should have had recourse to such an hypothesis to give a helping hand to Darwinian views is not only evidence of their weakness, but shows also wherein they are weak. It was, in fact, an admission that natural development will not account for the origination of seeds of plants. Now, if the generation of the different species of plants and trees cannot be ascribed to that process, it would seem to be wholly unreasonable to say that natural development, or natural selection, might effect the generation of different species of animals. It can by no means be conceded that the process in one case had no analogy to that in the other.

13. If, then, it should be asserted that the existence at any time of seed of any kind can only be due to the anterior or simultaneous origination, by creation, of the complete form of the plant or animal of which it is the seed, I maintain that, for the reasons above given, the principles of Darwinism cannot be legitimately adduced to controvert this assertion. Notwithstanding all that the advocates of that system may say, we shall be at liberty to attribute the origination of seed to the creation of perfect specimens of *each species*. This inference, which so far has been drawn from physical considerations, accords with the account of the creations of plants and animals given in the first chapter of Genesis. It is particularly to be noticed that in what is said in verses 11 and 12 respecting the creation of herbs and trees, the assertion is expressly made that " the seed of each is in itself after its kind." The way in which seed is thus spoken of in connexion with the creation of herbs and plants, is plainly consistent with the hypothesis that the seeds of different species have come into existence, not by development of one species from another, but by original creation of examples of each species. Although the above citation refers only to the vegetable kingdom, it may by analogy be taken to embrace the animal kingdom.

14. The Scriptural accounts of the creation of Adam from the dust of the ground, and of Eve from a rib of Adam, are quite consistent with the foregoing argument, according to which a single pair, at least, of the human race must have been *created*. It would be altogether unphilosophic to cavil at the specified modes of the creation, because, as already urged in Article 8, it is not possible to assign limits, whether as regards mode or extent, to the creative operations of the Framer of the Universe. It is worthy of notice that the possibility of such creations as those recorded respecting Adam and Eve was asserted by John the Baptist when he said,—" God is able of these stones to raise up children to Abraham." If the power of the Creator could be conceived of as having limits, there would cease to be meaning in the words, " Almighty," " Omnipotent." The particular modes of the miraculous creations of Adam and Eve have special significations, as indeed the miracles of Scripture always have. Adam, we are told, was made of the dust of the ground to indicate the terrestrial and unabiding character of the outward man ; and Eve was made of a bone of Adam to signify the intimate

relation that exists between husband and wife. Being originally created as to bodily form perfect man and perfect woman, they were unitedly and severally endowed with intellectual and moral qualities of the same kind as those of their Maker, and in these respects were created in His image.

15. If the foregoing arguments be good, any attempt to trace the origin of animals and of man to an oyster or a monad is altogether chimerical. Nature affords no data for an investigation of the generation of species. What Darwin says about *the generative effects* of "natural selection," "the survival of the strongest," &c., can only be empirical assertion, admitting of no verification from observation or experience. The kind of "development" the laws of which nature *does* afford the means of investigating, and which to my mind is the most wonderful of all natural operations,—more wonderful even than the construction of the heavens and the regulation of the movements of the heavenly bodies,—is that by which a plant or animal passes through successive stages from the seed to the complete organism. What, for instance, can be more astonishing than the development of the chick from the egg by the mere application of animal heat? The supporters of Darwinism, as Professor Huxley, are fond of adverting to the fact that at a certain stage the fœtus of a child differs but little from that of a puppy, as if such resemblance favoured the idea of development of species from a common origin. Here again, as it seems to me, is an instance of perverse judgment arising out of the admission of radically false principles. The similarity above mentioned gives no countenance to Darwinism, being only an example of *economy*, such as is characteristic of natural operations, according to which out of a general scheme or type of development, the most wonderful varieties of effect are produced, owing entirely to original differences existing within the small compass of the seed. How different, for instance, in the case just mentioned is the final development of one fœtus from that of the other! The study of the laws of these developments belongs to two distinct and most interesting departments of natural science, Organic Botany and Physiology, for the prosecution of which Nature gives ample data by presenting to our view, or offering for our researches, vegetable and animal life in all varieties of function, and all degrees of complexity, from "the hyssop that springeth out of the wall to the cedar of Lebanon," and from the encrinite and the oyster to the perfect organization of the human body.

16. I conclude by expressing the opinion, justified, I think, by the foregoing arguments, that so far from Darwinism being capable of giving support to Pantheistic and Atheistic Principles, it has no basis of its own to stand upon.

WYMAN AND SONS, PRINTERS, GREAT QUEEN STREET, LONDON, W.C.